Offbeat Travel

Exploring the unexpected and mysterious

Wayne P. Anderson

Wayne P. Anderson

© Wayne P. Anderson
www.venturebound.net
www.samplingtheworldsattractions.com

All rights reserved. No part of this book may be reproduced or transmitted in any form or by any means, electronic or mechanical or by any information or storage and retrieval system without permission in writing from the author or publisher.

Material from articles previously published in the Columbia Daily Tribune used with permission.

Published by AKA:yola / AKA-Publishing
Columbia, Missouri
www.akayola.com

Library of Congress
Anderson, Wayne P.
Offbeat Travel: Exploring the unexpected and mysterious
1. Travel 2. Family 3. History 4. Adventure
5. Ghosts 6. Oddities

ISBN: 978-1-936688-02-9

www.aka-publishing.com
www.akayola.com

Offbeat Travel

≈≈≈≈≈≈≈≈≈≈≈≈≈≈≈
Exploring the unexpected and mysterious
≈≈≈≈≈≈≈≈≈≈≈≈≈≈≈

Wayne P. Anderson

TABLE OF CONTENTS

	Page
Introduction	3

The honored dead
1. Unearthing Palermo — 7
2. Humanity on display in Body Worlds show — 10
3. Korean War Monument captures the conflict's costs — 13
4. Museum honors lost Oklahomans — 16
5. Andersonville Prison packs emotional punch — 19
6. Technology allows amazing look at mummies — 22
7. Titanic exhibit swamps viewers with emotion — 24

History from a different angle
8. Going 'Underground' in Seattle — 29
9. Former bordello still titillates the populace — 33
10. History marches on at Fort Leavenworth — 36
11. Little Rock Nine provides a lesson in human spirit — 39
12. Museum captures Lincoln's spirit — 43
13. Kellogg preached virtues of cereal and evils of sex — 46
14. Elgin Marbles still vex British-Greek relations — 49
15. Exploring India's 'caves' — 52
16. Was a black lawman the real Lone Ranger? — 55
17. Museum scrapes away mysteries of dentistry — 59

For real novelty visit any of the following
18. Would-be actors make ends meet on the street — 63
19. Trials at Old Bailey are lessons in law and order — 66
20. Gumshoes and trick shoes: Spy Museum amuses — 69
21. The Sheik's revenge — 72
22. Small in stature, big in history, the *Santa Maria* — 74
23. The rebirth of unclaimed baggage — 77
24. House-on-the-Rock, an impressive fortress — 80

Some family matters
25. Keeping a travel journal — 85
26. Close quarters test family ties — 88
27. Life on an English estate wasn't entirely romantic — 91
28. Two little angels make for a hellacious flight — 94
29. Bullfights! — 96

30. Bullfights through the eyes of a child	98
31. Familiar destination hosts travel wonders	100

Getting personal

32. Fear of flying	107
33. Sailing on the tall ships	109
34. Elmer Fudd, Rhino were difficult but memorable	113
35. I should have stayed home	115
36. Kentucky cave causes claustrophobic high	119
37. FBI study opens door to look at serial killers	121
38. Lumberjack museum lets writer step into Dad's past	124
39. Farm creates picture of life during Great Depression	126

Exploring the foreign scene

40. On a subject of modest importance	131
41. Trips to the Twilight Zone	134
42. Driving in Europe	137
43. Bribery part of the paycheck in corrupt countries	139
44. How to prevent and survive culture shock abroad	141
45. Meat, by any name, makes his meal	143

Experiencing the mysterious and unexplainable

46. New Orleans: Its unique dark side	147
47. St. Augustine's ghostly excursion	151
48. Savannah ghosts	155
49. Tower of London ghosts	159
50. London ghosts	163
51. Fort George	167
52. Chinese rites keep evil spirits in check	171
53. Ghosts of Williamsburg	174
54. Missouri boasts scores of scary tales	177

Introduction

Come join me in exploring some offbeat places. Imagine descending into a catacomb in Palermo where 8,000 bodies, dressed in their finest, await to be the first to welcome Christ's return. Or in exploring Andersonville Prison where food was so scarce it took seven Yanks to make a shadow. These are only two of the stories in the first section on the honored dead.

Or take a look at history from a different angle in the next section introducing you to the ancient caves of Ajanta and Ellora in India and the underground city of Seattle that for years had been forgotten. Section three explores some novelty sites including the trials at Old Bailey in London and a store in Alabama where thousands of lost items from air travel are for sale at bargain prices.

The family matters section will regale you with adventures with relatives and children including the story on living in a 9-by-9 tent with four little daughters. Section five on getting personal describes my emotional reactions on trips such as a failed canoe trip with my brother on the water-starved James River in North Dakota, overcoming the fear of flying, and crawling through a cave in Kentucky with 15 Elderhostelers.

Bribery, toilets, culture shock are all part of section six's exploration of the foreign scene. Seven ghost sites around the world are discussed in the final section, experiencing the mysterious and unexplainable. Included are the three outstanding ghost cities of the US: Savannah, St. Augustine and New Orleans.

All of these stories were first published on the travel pages of the *Columbia Daily Tribune*. On most expeditions I have been accompanied by my wife, Carla, who co-authored some of the stories and edited all of them never losing her delight in also coping with the unexpected.

Section 1

The Honored Dead

Unearthing Palermo

The upright, fully dressed bodies came as a shock to me. Earlier I had visited the catacombs of Rome and found them just a series of tunnels underground; the bodies were long gone. But in Palermo the bodies are there in all their decaying glory: 8,000 of them.

Usually I know what to expect when I visit a major tourist site. Although I am occasionally less than impressed, I am sometimes pleasantly surprised when the attraction is greater than its publicity. By and large, I usually have some idea of what it is I am about to see. I was totally unprepared for the Capuchin Catacombs of Palermo.

Some years back, my wife Carla and I were spending a delightful week in Sicily, enjoying the relics of the Roman and Greek empires and wonderful moonlight walks along the Mediterranean Sea. Another traveler recommended that we must be sure to see the "Museum of Death" in the Capuchin Convent.

We walked down the long staircase of the old church into a musty smelling hallway and what to our wondering eyes should appear but hundreds of mummified bodies dressed in clothes from the 17th and 18th centuries. It was a grotesque and outrageous scene, but nevertheless there was something fascinating about seeing bodies dressed in their personal best, standing in niches. They appeared to be staring back at us from sunken eyes embedded in parchment skin. The drying process has left the skin on the faces but has pulled them into horrifying expressions of terror and pain. Many seemed to be screaming—a massive silent scream.

There are a number of places in the world where the conditions are ideal for preserving bodies. I've seen mummies in Mexico, Peru, and Ireland. Palermo's climate and soil conditions are evidently some of the best for preserving bodies. When they first began the practice, the bodies were laid out in the Catacombs and allowed to dehydrate. They were then washed in vinegar, clothed in their finest and placed on and in the walls. I understand that later the method of embalming was modified and many of the bodies were cured for months in a salt solution.

We were told two stories as to why the bodies were there dressed and standing as if in anticipation of some great event. The first story held that these were devoted believers who wanted to be ready when Christ returned and to be the first to welcome him at the time of the resurrection of the body.

The second story, and the one I heard later, is probably the true reason the practice started. In the 16th century the local priests decided to mummify the body of the holy monk, Brother Silvestro. They felt this would be a great way to preserve his body so they could pray to him after his death. Initially only monks were preserved in this way and placed in the Catacombs. Other citizens of Palermo who heard of this felt this would be a good way to have their loved ones where they could come to visit them and grieve their loss.

Even in death, there were signs that not all people were seen as equals. There are separate sections for priests, men, women, children and professionals. The most "important" people — the lawyers, doctors, and landowners — are in the better-lighted passageways. Many of them have black jackets and some wear top hats. Two and three hundred years, however, even in a dry cool area has left their clothes looking weathered and aged. As you move deeper into the Catacombs the corridors become darker and cooler and the mummies and their clothes are in even poorer condition. The clothes are definitely dilapidated and the bodies are showing greater signs of decomposition. We notice here some fingers missing, and there a hand.

Many of the women are lying in shelves cut into the stone walls. Some of them are dressed in their wedding dresses. Children are often grouped in alcoves, smallest in front. In places the bodies are floor to ceiling, wall to wall. Most of those standing are attached to the wall in some way: hooks, ropes, perhaps even nailed.

Offbeat Travel

The most striking, and for us emotionally touching, body is that of a two-year-old girl who is perfectly preserved and who looks like she is asleep in her crib. The doctor who embalmed her died before anyone could learn his secret formula.

Photo taking is not allowed. But you are left with a feeling that somehow taking pictures would be an invasion of their privacy even greater than what you've just committed walking amongst them. Their facial expressions are such that you feel they wouldn't want the world to see them like this.

The Italian government forbid the process in 1881, and only a few bodies have been added by special permission since that date. Not the most pleasant tourist attraction to visit, but certainly one of the most unusual and memorable.

Humanity on Display in Body Worlds Show
WAYNE AND CARLA ANDERSON

With all of his muscles and body parts in vivid natural color, a man stands carrying his folded skin draped across his arm. With both figures similarly stripped of skin and organs exposed, another man on a rearing horse holds the horse's brain in one hand and his own brain, proportionately larger, in another. This pair took workers 3½ years to finish.

We were spending the day at the Body Worlds traveling exhibition of 25 plastinated real human bodies in active poses along with 200 healthy and diseased organs in cases, all displayed with detailed descriptions, at the Science Museum on the campus of the University of California, Los Angeles.

The exhibition came as a complete surprise to us, as we had read nothing about it beforehand. We are both fascinated by what German anatomist Gunther von Hagens has been able to do in displaying the systems and parts of the human body. One exhibit, for example, focuses on a man's circulatory system standing by itself, isolated from the rest of the body.

But reactions vary. Wayne is uneasy with what he is seeing, feeling it is on the edge of horrific. Carla is impressed by how beautiful but fragile some of the figures are in their artistic poses as they teach us about ourselves.

As we later learn, the exhibition has raised some controversy. For example, one of the figures causing consternation for some visitors shows a terminally ill woman, who was eight months pregnant, her unborn fetus visible.

One display, which some visitors note as bordering on the sensational, depicts a runner with his muscles flaring out around him as if his speed is stripping them from his body. A woman swimmer's body is split in half, the halves swimming away from each other.

We agreed that a breakthrough has occurred in educating professionals and laymen about human physiology and on the effect such displays have on changing habits and lifestyle choices.

An example is a display of the lungs of a smoker and nonsmoker, where some visitors have left their cigarettes. Other exhibits show artificial hip joints, a diseased heart, a liver with cirrhosis and the brain of someone who had Alzheimer's.

Our entrance was timed because so many people were flooding to see the exhibit that only a certain number could enter at a time. The sound of the crowd was muted, no loud talking or laughter. Visitors were treating the displays seriously and respectfully.

In the late 1970s, von Hagens developed a method of turning a human body into plastic to prevent decay. He removed the bodily liquids and fats using vacuum pressure and replaced them with resins and elastic substances. Curing with light, heat and gases made the parts rigid and permanent. The method also allowed him to put the bodies into various action-oriented positions, such as the basketball and soccer players.

We saw the exhibition five years ago and had decided not to write about it, but we kept seeing announcements of where it has been, where it is and where it will be next. The exhibition, first shown in 1995 in Tokyo, became so popular that Body Worlds 2 and 3 began in 2005 and 2006 with similar exhibits so that there can be showings in three places at once. More than 20 million viewers have seen these exhibits, making them the most popular special exhibitions in the world.

In the two later exhibitions, von Hagens created more female figures in response to popular demand. In the first exhibition he concentrated his efforts more on male figures to avoid possible censure about women's bodies on display.

Controversy has continued to swirl around the exhibition. There are no faces on the anonymous bodies, but the underlying muscles remain intact. Where do the bodies come from? Von Hagens has been accused of using executed prisoners and hospital patients, but he maintains that all donors gave informed consent.

The list of donors volunteering their bodies after death grows with every exhibition, indicating that many people see the project as worthy of support or possibly that some might want their moment of fame, even if it is anonymous.

There have been some negative reactions, especially from fellow anatomists, one of whom called it, "Dr. Death and his traveling freak show." Von Hagens has been accused of showing disrespect for the dead and of sensationalism. He believed that good teachers find ways to "dress up" what they are trying to explain to attract and maintain students' attention. The country that has given him the most static has been his home country of Germany, where several cities attempted to block his show.

Visitors' reactions to Body Worlds generally have been favorable, with more than 80 percent in an independent poll giving it a "good" or "very good" rating. The exhibitions are currently in Dallas, Montreal and Phoenix, and this summer they will be in Portland, Ore., and Charlotte, N.C. Audio guides are available.

If imitation is the sincerest form of flattery, there is a lot of flattery out there, with at least seven similar exhibitions around the world developed by competitors. For more information, visit the Web site at www.bodyworlds.com.

Korean War Monument Captures the Conflict's Costs

The Korean War Veterans Memorial includes stainless-steel sculptures of 19 servicemen from the Army, Navy, Air Force and Marines.

WASHINGTON, D.C. - The Korean War Veterans Memorial had the greatest emotional impact on me when I recently visited three war monuments on the Washington Mall. To the west of the Washington Monument and close to the Lincoln Memorial, the three monuments honor the sacrifices of three generations of American soldiers in three wars: World War II, in which 400,000 died; the Vietnam War, in which 58,245 died; and the Korean War, in which 50,000 died.

The Korean War from 1950 to 1953 is the conflict my high school classmates served in; some died, and several of my friends were never quite the same again. At least two had post-traumatic stress disorder, a diagnosis that was not officially made until sometime after the Vietnam War. The sadly thoughtful homecoming of my classmates and friends was in contrast to the eagerness with which they marched off to the conflict in Korea.

When I started graduate school at the University of Missouri in 1954, some of my fellow students were veterans of that conflict, and later, as a Veterans Administration hospital psychologist, I listened to my patients' stories of the winter retreat in which so many of our soldiers died.

Korea is sometimes called our forgotten war. For a considerable time, it did not seem to be thought of as something to memorialize despite the fact that 5.7 million of our men and women would eventually serve in that arena. Not until 1986 did Congress authorize the memorial, and not until 1995 did President Bill Clinton along with Kim Young Sam, president of the Republic of Korea, dedicate the memorial on the 42nd anniversary of the armistice.

In contrast to the much larger World War II monument, the Korean War monument brings that conflict's memory alive by giving us the sense that real people suffered and died in the war. The chief sculptor, Frank Gaylord, who served in World War II, has given us 19 stainless-steel servicemen on patrol walking across a field of scrubby juniper bushes. Representing various ethnic groups in the Army, Navy, Air Force and Marines, they carry a variety of weapons - M-1 carbines, M-14 rifles and a BAR - and one man carries the radio. They are ready for action in a dangerous situation. Their faces are wary and strained - the faces of men who have seen death and destruction. Heavy ponchos that appear to be blowing in the wind protect them from the fierce weather of Korea.

On a black 164-foot-long graphite wall beside the cautious troops, the artist Louis Nelson has created a mural of 2,500 faces of men and women who provided support for the ground troops. Here are the surgeons, stretcher bearers, bridge builders and others needed to conduct a war. The realistic images, taken from photographs in the military archives, have been sandblasted in photographic detail into the wall. The 19 steel soldiers' images are reflected in the black, glossy wall, doubling their number to 38, a symbolic reference to the 38th parallel that divides North Korea and South Korea.

Nearby is the "Pool of Remembrance" showing the number of U.S. and U.N. troops who died, were wounded, captured or missing in action. Two inscriptions are especially poignant: "Our nation honors her sons and daughters who answered the call to defend a country they never knew and a people they never met" and, inlaid in silver, "Freedom is Not Free."

Except for Dec. 25, park rangers give daily talks and answer questions. A bookstore at the Lincoln Memorial sells items about the memorial and the Korean War. For more information, visit www.nps.gov/kowa.

Wayne P. Anderson

Museum Honors Lost Oklahomans

With 300,000 visitors a year, the Oklahoma City National Memorial Center Museum is one of America's most visited sites. Built in the wake of the terrorist bombing of the Murrah Federal Building in 1995, where 168 people died and 700 were injured.

The reflecting pool with chairs on the right

As we entered through one of the gates of time overlooking the reflecting pool, we were met by a park ranger who explained what we were seeing. Each of the 168 lighted chairs spaced along the pool represents someone who died. Nineteen of the chairs are smaller than the rest. They represent children.

The memorial museum covers three floors of one end of the former Journal Record Building, which was also damaged in the explosion. We started the tour on the third floor, where the scene is set by taking us to the hour before 9 a.m. on April 19, 1995.

It is a peaceful day. We see scenes of the city and what is happening outside and inside the building. Next, we enter a quiet room where the one recording made that morning is played. A case is being brought for permission to use groundwater from under a home to bottle water for sale. Two minutes into the meeting there is an explosion, the room goes dark, and then the faces of the 168 people killed in the explosion are flashed onto the wall. It took our breath away.

Appearing on a screen in the next room are images of chaos and destruction taken from a helicopter when it still was not known exactly what had happened. In the background we hear police and emergency calls and reporters describing what they see. Hovering over all is a sense of confusion.

As we pass through the debris-filled rooms on the third floor, we listen to comments by three groups of people: those who survived the immediate explosion and destruction, those who lost loved ones in the explosion and the first responders who dug the bodies out and cared for the injured and dying. The interviews on the large screen televisions are high definition, which gives scenes an almost 3-D quality.

Stories from survivors focus on how they helped and were helped. One blind man led some others out because the air was so filled with smoke they couldn't find their way out and he could. Many stories stressed how people acted bravely and cooperated well.

The most horrendous stories come from those trapped under the rubble. They had to talk themselves into remaining calm: "I'm still alive; I can't quit; I can't fall asleep."

All felt the bombing had changed their lives. A follow-up study found 34 percent still suffered from post-traumatic stress disorder years later. Some mentioned in their interviews that they felt surviving the incident had made them stronger.

Visitors continue to place mementoes on the wall outside the Oklahoma City bombing.

Offbeat Travel

Andersonville Prison Packs Emotional Punch

"It took seven of us to make a shadow." - Civil War prisoner at Andersonville Prison

Some famous places have so much negative energy it is difficult to tout them as attractions. It took me several days after I visited the Confederate prison camp at Andersonville, Ga., before I could put my reactions on paper.

Andersonville, now a National Historic Site under the National Park Service, was opened in 1998 as a memorial to all U.S. prisoners of war from all the wars we have fought.

Three major parts to the site include the visitors' center, the field on which the 45,000 Union prisoners were held, and the graveyard, which is not only a burial site for the dead of Andersonville but a national cemetery.

The museum at the visitors' center builds a sense of what it would be like to be a prisoner by using narrow display areas with sudden bends. Several of the small POW cells from various conflicts include the irons used to restrain the prisoners.

Displays from all wars in which Americans were held captive include information on civilians who were captives. Some displays show how our own government imprisoned American Indians during the Indian wars, Germans in World War I and the Japanese in World War II.

Two movies in the visitors' center were especially powerful. A 20-minute film had re-enactors using words taken from letters and diaries of the prisoners held at Andersonville. They tell us of the horrible conditions that killed so many: the bad water, the disease, the brutality, the starvation. The images their words painted were shocking, showing how cruelly man can treat man.

In the movie, the story is told of the Raiders, a group of Union soldiers who bullied, killed and generally ran roughshod over the others. The other prisoners eventually organized, had the group arrested, held a trial and received permission to hang the six ringleaders.

Originally intended for 10,000 prisoners, Andersonville eventually held 45,000. Gen. Ulysses Grant had stopped the prisoner exchange program for two reasons. First, the South was killing any black soldiers captured or returning them as property to their original owners. Second, as soon as a Confederate soldier was returned, he went back into battle.

Grant figured he couldn't get ahead of the game if that was the way the South was going to play it. A Union prisoner could gain his freedom if he would sign up to fight for the Confederacy; few did.

Food supplies were short for the South; even their own troops were not getting enough to eat. Viewing the pictures taken after the prisoners were freed made me wonder how men so emaciated could have survived. Some 13,000 soldiers died in the camp during its two years of operation.

The camp is mostly empty ground with markers to show where the walls and the deadline, about 10 feet inside the walls, were. Any prisoner crossing the deadline was shot. One corner of the 26-acre area has a wall with a guard tower and some ragged tarps set up as tents to illustrate living conditions.

The letters indicated some men simply gave up, turned their faces to the wall and died. It was pointed out in one of the displays in the visitors' center that this also happened with our Japanese prisoners.

One large display of multiple TV screens focuses on stories of the families at home as told by survivors from World War II, the Korean and Vietnam wars. Some commentaries are by the survivors, several of whom were prisoners for seven years, but most are by wives, mothers and children of what it was like not to know whether their loved ones were living or dead, the joy of learning they were alive and then the anxiety of wondering whether they would survive. Some, of course, did not. One particularly poignant story was of a man whose girlfriend's picture kept him alive, only for him later to learn she had married someone else.

The final place to visit is the graveyard, where the first thing I saw was thousands of small headstones only an inch apart. Most men had been buried in mass graves with only a numbered marker.

One of the prisoners kept secret records of which men were buried in which mass graves. After the war, he and Clara Barton, founder of the American Red Cross, went back and had individual headstones placed.

A park ranger said they have 90,000 visitors a year, but the number is falling because so many veterans of World War II who came as visitors are dying.

This is a moving, well-done memorial. Visitors can reach it by traveling about 30 miles off Interstate 75 south of Macon, Ga.

Wayne P. Anderson

Technology Allows Amazing Look at Mummies

So this 3-D mummy is coming at me feet-first, and as I prepare to duck, the feet start to dissolve so that I can follow the intricate structure of the body all the way to the top of the head. I was sitting in a packed theater at the British Museum in London in March of 05 watching the results of a CT scanner reconstruction of the body of a 3,000-year-old priest, Nesperennub, from the temple of Khons.

A Computerized Axial Tomography scan - also called a CT or CAT scan - takes pictures internally and externally of a body and puts them together using a computer.

This use of cutting-edge technology will make science museums even more entertaining than they have been in the past. Now a mummy no longer needs to be destroyed by unwrapping it in order for curious scientists to make a medical diagnosis, check age and physical condition at death or even do a crime-scene analysis.

Nesperennub, who lived around 800 B.C., was the first mummy to undergo a "virtual unwrapping" with the use of a CT scanner. Included in the film is the clever reconstruction of his face by a forensic anthropologist. An actor chosen for similar looks re-enacted scenes from the life of a priest of Egypt. During those times, being a priest was a pretty cushy deal and sure beat pulling giant stones up an incline to build a pyramid.

"Mummy: The Inside Story" had three acts. First, the crowd entered an introductory area, where we were given a presentation on how a mummy was prepared and some facts about ancient Egypt. Demonstrations showed how the brain was stirred with a probe and removed. It was then discarded, because it was not considered a very important organ. Egyptians thought the heart did the thinking. The process of preservation was also illustrated.

A short film showed us how mummies in the past were destroyed by investigators seeking to learn more about them. The practice was stopped, and anthropologists have been waiting for techniques to be developed that would allow the noninvasive investigation of these human time capsules.

We next entered a specially designed theater with a curved screen and stereo projection equipment. The mummy was soon floating right in front of us in gross nonliving color. How did he die? What was his age? How could the experts be sure it was a man? These were the kind of questions they answered as they took us on our "virtual tour."

The final room of the exhibition held Nesperennub's mummy in his painted coffin along with a multitude of artifacts we had just seen in the 3D movie.

The show pulled large crowds who waited hours for their turn in the theater. The addition of 3-D to virtual reality makes this a thrilling experience worth the wait.

The British Museum has the largest collection of Egyptian mummies and other artifacts outside of Cairo. A selection of 140 items has been making a tour of American and Canadian museums the past couple of years. As I write this, the show "Mummies: Death and the Afterlife in Ancient Egypt" is in Santa Ana, Calif. Six of the mummies in the collection will be undergoing CT scans, which I suspect means that a similar show to the one I saw in London will should soon be available in American museums.

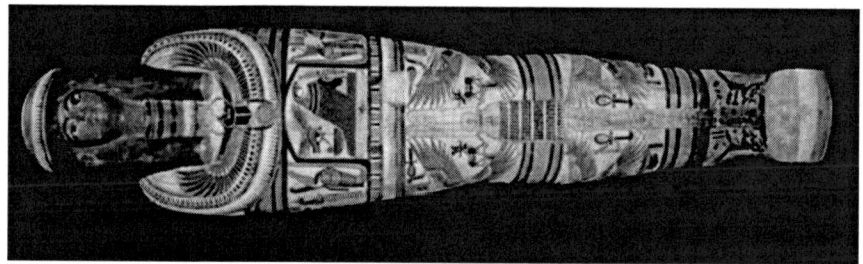

Nesperennub

Wayne P. Anderson

Titanic Exhibit Swamps Viewer with Emotions
WAYNE AND CARLA ANDERSON

The *Titanic*: The Artifact Exhibition has been making the rounds in cities such as Denver, San Francisco and Toronto, recording an attendance of more than 18 million people. Slightly different versions are now in Las Vegas and Galveston, Texas. When we saw the exhibition several years ago at the Science Museum in London, we found it emotionally charged and enlightening.

The *Titanic*, a floating palace owned by the White Star Line, was considered to be unsinkable when it started its maiden voyage. On a calm April night in 1912, it struck an iceberg and sank into the North Atlantic.

Molly Brown, women's rights advocate, and many business leaders such as John Jacob Astor and Benjamin Guggenheim were aboard, which added to the publicity the sinking received from reporters. This tragic story captured the public imagination and has been told in at least eight movies and featured in eight others.

It wasn't until the 1980s that equipment and techniques were developed that allowed recovery of

Visitors to the *Titanic* exhibit are each given a boarding pass with information about one of the passengers. At the end of the tour, they find out whether the passengers survived.

items from the wreck, which was almost 2½ miles below the surface. In the 1990s, RMS Titanic Inc. made recovery expeditions to the vessel's site and recovered more than 6,000 artifacts from the wreck.

What made the exhibit so emotionally charged were the methods used to personalize the tour. Visitors are given an audio tour that features original music, narration, sound effects and interviews with survivors.

Just as important for the emotional effect, as we entered we were each given a boarding pass allowing us to identify with one of the passengers. It explained why that person was on board and what class passage each had taken. We were told that at the end we would find out whether we were among the 1,523 passengers who died or were one of the 705 who survived. Immediately we were concerned if "we" had made it.

For example, Carla was given the card for Allison "Bess" Hudson, a 25-year-old mother of two from Chesterville, Ontario, traveling on a first-class ticket. She was accompanying her husband on business, and she had made a side trip to Scotland, where she selected furniture for their home and recruited new household staff for their two residences.

There was a life-size recreation of a first-class cabin and accommodations so we could see how the rich lived and a third-class hallway and multiple-person cabin so we could see the contrast. The dinnerware looked new, and many of the personal belongings, such as jewelry, shoes, razors and banknotes, looked well-preserved.

It was also interesting to see how many of the stories highlighted were about people who had booked another trip: They had not planned to be on the *Titanic*, but circumstances put them there.

For example, "Marion Meanwell booked passage on *Titanic's* maiden voyage when a coal strike delayed her scheduled trip on the *Majestic*. Her inspection card shows *Majestic* crossed out and replaced with the name of the doomed *Titanic*. Marion Meanwell did not survive." The captain's trip also was unplanned; he had expected to retire but was talked into making this his last voyage.

Of course, some people were lucky and missed the boat, and some of their stories also were told.

The iceberg room added a physical experience to the tragedy with its great block of ice that let us get a small sense of what it was like to be in the freezing water of the North Atlantic.

After getting into our respective roles as passengers, when we got to the Memorial Gallery, where lists on a wall recorded who survived and who did not; we were eager to find out if we had made it. We were saddened to learn we both had died. Bess Hudson could have gotten on a boat with her son, but as her husband and daughter were missing, she left her son with the governess and went looking for her husband. She died in a swamped boat. Only her son survived.

"Ghosts of the Abyss," an IMAX movie that accompanies the exhibition, gives a detailed account of the process of finding and then recovering the items. That an exhibition of this type has been put together is remarkable.

Section 2

History from a Different Angle

Offbeat Travel

Going 'Underground' in Seattle
Tour Reveals Historic City's Long-Forgotten Past

Taking the popular walking tour "Underground Seattle" is like being dropped into a time capsule of the late 19th and early 20th centuries.

My wife, Carla, and I took a guided tour with 50 other people and found the commentary to be funnier than most comedy routines that we've heard. This was partly because the people of Seattle have no sense of shame about their city's history, and all of their mistakes and crooked citizens are grist for the humor mill.

Pioneer Square is the old section of town that has been preserved on the National Register of Historic Places. Underneath this part of town we walked the streets and into the rooms that had been "lost" for many years.

Seattleites are a laid-back group who take pride in having been settled by men driven by greed. The early entrepreneurs who built the West Coast port city took the short-term, quick-dollar approach. As a result, the original city was poorly planned and developed.

Being on a tidal plain, objects had a tendency to sink into the ground. Anything available was used to fill in holes, and because there was a lumber mill downtown, sawdust was often used along with ballast from ships coming up from San Francisco. Potholes became so large they were given names, and certain streets were avoided because horses with their wagons had been lost in the giant cavities.

Another interesting problem that arose involved the popularity in 1860s of the new flush toilet that had been invented in England by Thomas Crapper. Twice a day, when the tide came in, the sewers flowed backward and the toilets became geysers. In a number of places we saw old toilets featured as museum items.

Most people considered it a blessing when the original city was burned down in the Great Seattle Fire of 1887. This was partly as a result of the failure of the city to have any organized fire department. Some of the businessmen had private arrangements, but the firefighters' performance was like something out of a silent comedy and only ensured that the fire would do a complete job.

Rather than use the fire as an opportunity to improve things, the conditions temporarily became worse. The businessmen were in a hurry to get back to making money, so, although they built with brick, they did it on the same level as the old flood plain. The city of Seattle, however, owned the streets and decided it would be better if they were 8 to 35 feet higher than they had been. That meant the storefronts and sidewalks were below the level at which traffic passed by. To go from the sidewalk on one side of the street to the sidewalk on the next street meant climbing up a ladder, walking across the street and climbing a ladder down into the next sidewalk.

Remember, this was a time when women wore hoop-skirts and 20 pounds of petticoats. How they got up the ladders carrying their purchases can only be imagined. Our guide said men always seemed eager to hold a ladder, given that the glimpse of an ankle or, heaven forbid, a lady's calf, was very titillating.

Drunks had a problem with falling off the street down to the sidewalk, some being killed. Our guide said 18 deaths were reported. On several occasions, horses pulling carts fell off the streets onto the sidewalks and smashed the windows of the businesses below.

This led businessmen to reconsider their earlier decision, and they built a brick sidewalk even with the street and turned the second stories of their buildings into the first floor. Skylights were built on the corners to give light to the sidewalks below.

Eventually, the underground city that was created by this move was forgotten. There was a brief period during Prohibition when parts of the lower area were turned into speakeasies, but in the 1930s they lapsed into a forgotten area that existed only in rumors.

In 1954, the area was to be torn down, but journalist Bill Speidel, encouraged by his wife, Shirley, figured that if 25 people complaining about topless go-go dancers could get a law passed forbidding their performances, he could get enough people interested in saving an important area of town. As Bill said, "I can do anything Shirley makes up her mind that I can do."

Under his leadership, Pioneer Square was placed on the National Register of Historic Buildings, and he began giving tours of the underground that have grown in popularity over the years. The 90-minute tours run on the hour, and if you don't buy your ticket early, you wait for the next tour in a pleasant shop surrounded by pictures and stories of the scoundrels and heroes who founded the city.

While I was in Seattle, I met a retired pipe welder named JT who had worked in the underground area in 1956 when natural gas was brought into town. He worked in parts of the underground that are not on the tour. These streets and buildings were bricked up. JT said they had to break down walls to get the pipes laid. Among other things they found were a casket with a well preserved corpse in it and baggage that had been left by immigrants who had come into the area, complete with their old fashioned clothes, family pictures and letters. There were also gold and silver coins more than 100 years old. He believes much of this remains untouched.

A part of the history of Pioneer Square concerns trees. There were thousands of giant trees on the cliffs surrounding Seattle, and they needed to be cleared. San Francisco needed lumber, so the trees were cut and a skid road made of tree trunks was built so the trees could be slid down to the sawmill.

Later Skid Road became the haunt of criminals, alcoholics and ladies of the night. The name not only stuck for Seattle but was used in other cities around the country for any place that fell into disrepair and harbored drunks and prostitutes.

A vacation in Seattle wouldn't be complete without a visit to Pike Place Market, a short walk from Pioneer Square. If you don't like walking, free buses run up the street. Pike Place Market is famous for its seafood markets and restaurants, but the stalls have a wide variety of items for sale. The market is as close in nature as I have seen in this country to the markets in European cities.

You can get more information about Seattle, by e-mail, from seattle@where-magazine.com, or point your browser to www.seeseattle.org, or call the visitors bureau at (206) 461-5840.

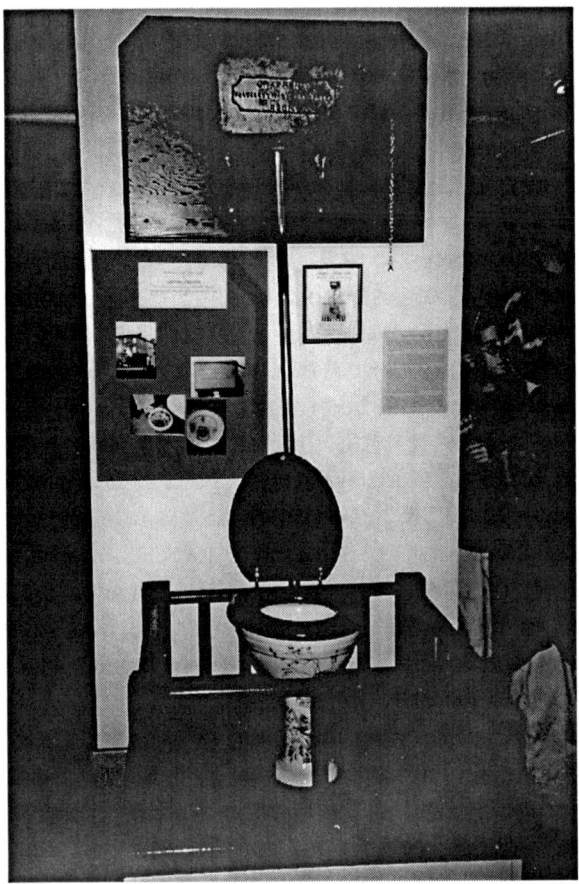

The new flush toilet that became a geyser when the tide came in

Offbeat Travel

Former Bordello Still Titillates the Populace

FORT SMITH, Ark. - This town turned out to be much bigger than my wife, Carla, and I expected. When we finally found the visitor center, it turned out to be called Miss Laura's Brothel. In 1973, the building was placed on the National Register of Historic Places, the only former brothel so honored.

The two older lady guides were just starting their enthusiastic tour of the facility as we came in. Our two volunteer guides took a great deal of pleasure in conducting the tour, especially because we were all adults and they didn't have to circle around and make veiled references to what the business here had been.

The local men at the time saw Miss Laura's as the quality place; her girls were the most refined and healthiest. I asked if that meant free of sexually transmitted diseases, and the guide said no. They were free of tuberculosis. If a case of TB was found, a house was closed down.

The stained-glass windows at Miss Laura's, a former brothel that now serves as the Fort Smith, Ark, visitor's center, have been restored or replaced with similar works.

Girls always greeted customers fully dressed in a parlor furnished with some of the best designed and constructed furniture of the period. This sent the message that this was a quality establishment. The quality was also reflected in the price of the services, which was $3 - at other places on the row; the price was only $1. Despite the aura of quality, however, the women were treated as outcasts by the community and were virtually prisoners in their houses.

Laura Zeigler opened River Front Hotel in 1903 with money she borrowed from a local banker. She had nine girls working for her, and the place became one of the most celebrated bordellos in the Southwest. Business was so good that she was able to pay off the loan in 17 months.

Copies of the original wallpaper have been created; the stained-glass windows have been restored or good copies provided. Each of the working girls' rooms is decorated in the original style. As I looked at the rooms, I thought this must have been a step up in bedroom décor for many of the customers. Mannequins dressed in the style of the period are in several of the rooms. The furnishings are in Victorian style and similar to the ones used by Miss Laura in the original building.

Pictures of some of the original occupants are on the walls, and several glass cases display objects of the period. This includes a .22-caliber Smith and Wesson revolver that was similar to the kind some girls kept in their rooms as protection against rowdy customers. On the transoms of the rooms are the names of the more memorable women who worked here.

Singing, dancing and gambling were also part of the allure. When there was an especially good month, Miss Laura chilled champagne in an upstairs bathtub and served it free to her customers, many of whom were prominent local figures.

In January 1910, an oil storage tank exploded, setting a number of brothels on fire and causing many of the scantily clad ladies and their customers to rush out into the street. The incident became known as "the night of the lingerie parade."

In 1924, prostitution became illegal, and the houses officially went out of business. This is the only surviving building of the seven brothels that once existed in the area - two burned down, and others were demolished. In 1992, it became the Fort Smith visitor center operated by volunteers.

Before Miss Laura's time, there was a great disproportion of men to women. In the first half of the 1800s, it might have been 100-to-1. This not only resulted in good business for brothels, but it was not unusual for a man to take a working girl for his wife.

A tornado in 1996 ripped the roof off the building, but it has been restored and gives visitors a firsthand view of how some of those with money lived in the early 1900s.

Wayne P. Anderson

History Marches on at Fort Leavenworth

LEAVENWORTH, Kan. - Bad guys and good guys: Leavenworth has seen more than its fair share of both among its pioneers, adventurers and military heroes.

Our daughter, Debra, who had once been stationed as an officer at Fort Leavenworth, took my wife, Carla, and me on a tour of this fort, which is the oldest fort in continuous service west of the Mississippi.

We had to show picture IDs to enter the base, and if we hadn't been with our daughter, our car would have been closely checked for whatever is forbidden these days.

First, we went to the Frontier Army Museum and then to the various important points of historical interest. Our conclusion - this is one history-packed base.

Lewis and Clark had stopped in this area before a fort was established. Beginning in 1827 the Army's role here was to keep peace among the various American Indian tribes and the increasing number of settlers heading west.

The pioneers moving on the Oregon Trail and commercial wagons traveling on the Santa Fe Trail passed through here. At one point near the river, the swales - ruts dug into the landscape by wagons - are still visible.

Of the 14 films about the area's history available, we chose one on the forts of Kansas, which gave us a 34-minute story of what they were like and what has happened to them. Forts were very much needed, as white settlers met with resistance as they took away the homeland and the livelihood of the American Indians.

A second short film on the Hunt Club showed locals in fancy black and red coats riding after their pack of dogs.

In the museum, the red sled of Gen. George Custer, who was stationed here, sat between the sled of Gen. Jonathan Wainwright and the special carriage used by Abraham Lincoln when he stopped in the area in 1859 for a week to campaign for the presidency. Lincoln made a good impression here, even among the slave owners. He seemed like "down-home folks" and was especially noted for spinning amusing stories to illustrate his points.

Among good guys who spent time in Leavenworth were William "Buffalo Bill" Cody, James "Wild Bill" Hickok and Martha Jane "Calamity Jane" Burke.

A striking statue in a fountain, "Buffalo Soldier," pays homage to the two regiments of black soldiers who were a mainstay during the Indian Wars. A national cemetery with 31,300 graves of veterans dates from the Indian Wars to the present day.

The school that was to become the U.S. Army Command and General Staff College, where my son-in-law is an instructor, was established in 1881 by Gen. William Tecumseh Sherman.

Many famous people not only from the United States but also from many other countries have received their advanced officer training here.

Americans include George C. Marshall, President Dwight D. Eisenhower, Gen. Douglas MacArthur, Gen. Colin Powell and Gen. George Patton. Our son-in-law took us through the new state-of-the-art instruction facilities that have just opened.

Who were the bad guys? Long before I knew they had a fort and command college here, I had heard of Leavenworth as where the serious criminals were locked up. My daughter indicated there really are four prisons in the area, none of which you can visit as a tourist.

The military prison at the fort, formally called the United States Disciplinary Barracks, was established in 1875. A new barracks, built in 2002 and housing 521 prisoners, is the only maximum-security prison in the U.S. Department of Defense that holds inmates from all branches of the service.

Across the street from the fort is Leavenworth's most famous prison, the United States Penitentiary that has held such notables as Al Capone, "Machine Gun" Kelly and Robert Stroud, who was known as the "Birdman of Alcatraz." Until 2005 it was the largest maximum-security prison in the country, but now is a medium-security prison housing 2,300 prisoners.

The Corrections Corp. of America Leavenworth, a private prison, is mostly used to hold prisoners awaiting trial. Just south of Leavenworth is the Kansas state penitentiary, now officially named the Lansing Correctional Facility, which houses 2,445 inmates.

Leavenworth is only a short distance north of Kansas City on the Kansas side of the Missouri River. In spite of the car checks when entering, guests are welcome to visit the fort, tour the historic sites on the base and view the prisons in the area from the outside.

"Buffalo Soldier"

Little Rock Nine Provides a Lesson in Human Spirit
CARLA AND WAYNE ANDERSON

LITTLE ROCK, Ark. - "The whole nation took one giant step forward," said Melba Beals, one of the Little Rock Nine, the black students who were escorted by the Army's 101st Airborne to integrate Little Rock's Central High School on Sept. 25, 1957.

The Little Rock Nine Memorial, life-size statues of the students on the grounds of Arkansas Capitol, seems to us an apology and a step toward atonement for an embarrassing event in our country's history.

Statues of the Little Rock Nine stand on the lawn of the Arkansas Capitol in Little Rock. 2007 marks the 50th anniversary of the integration of Little Rock's Central High School.

In February we visited Little Rock in this 50th anniversary year to learn more about what happened here that caused a national crisis and earned the town international attention.

When the nine students returned to visit the school in 1987, they were treated as heroes. However, during the school year of 1957-58 they struggled against many attacks from student and adult segregationists.

Wayne P. Anderson

Central High School, once named "America's Most Beautiful High School," is now a National Historic Site. Across the street from the high school, which had more than 2,000 students in 1957, is a small Mobil gas station that has become the visitor center.

On a small old-fashioned black-and-white television is a constantly running tape of the event. Angry mobs of about 400 whites gathered as the students prepared to enter the school. The dress of Elizabeth Eckford, one of the nine threatened students, became so drenched with spit she could wring it out.

Gov. Orval Faubus sent in the Arkansas National Guard to block the students' entrance under the premise that soldiers were needed to prevent rioting and that the best way to prevent rioting was to keep black students out of the school.

When President Dwight Eisenhower failed to get Faubus' cooperation in integrating the school, he nationalized the Arkansas National Guard and sent in 101st Airborne soldiers to escort and protect the nine black students.

The students indicated they felt noticeably better protected by those soldiers than by the Arkansas National Guard that replaced some of them. Eckford said her escort followed 11 paces behind and did not enter classrooms or the showers.

In the showers is where some of the physical abuse occurred. The boys were hit with wet, knotted towels, and the girls were scalded in the showers when the white girls flushed all of the toilets simultaneously.

The black students were insulted and threatened, kicked and tripped and shoved in the halls and against lockers. Eckford took to carrying her notebook in front of her with pins sticking slightly out, which did, after the first attack, avert further frontal attacks. Their books were stolen and ripped. Pencils and spitballs were thrown at them. Ink was squirted on their clothes.

Melba Beals' left eye was injured when acid was thrown at her. The damage was lessened as her guard immediately threw water on her face. She was pushed onto broken glass in gym class. She noted that each day she worried, "Who's going to hit me today?

Will someone throw hot soup on me today? Will it be greasy and ruin the dress my grandmother made for me?"

Most of the white students who tried to befriend the black students were threatened by the extremist students and withdrew their help. Teachers didn't want to take reports of abuse, and the principal said the school would take action only if an attack were witnessed by a teacher.

For the black students to take defensive or retaliatory action would have meant being kicked out of school. The normally friendly Minnijean Brown Trickey was expelled when she dumped hot chili on two harassing boys who were not punished.

The nine were counseled daily and encouraged to be nonviolent by Daisy Bates, president of the state chapter of the National Association for the Advancement of Colored People and co-publisher of the Arkansas State Press.

Ernest Green, the first black student to graduate from Central, said, "I knew that I had accomplished what I'd come there for. I had cracked the wall."

He calmly noted, "It's been an interesting year. I've had a course in human relations firsthand."

On the old-fashioned television, visitors can relive the controversy and get an appreciation for the tremendous stress that was placed on the black students. They needed armed protection for the whole year.

In defiance of national orders, the school was closed the next year. As we watched, we had the feeling that integration of schools would have taken much longer if we had not had television reports to show the nation what was happening.

On a larger color television are interviews with people who were involved at the time in the struggle to eliminate separate systems of education for blacks and whites. We find it difficult at this distance in time to understand the strong emotions that were involved in keeping blacks out of white schools.

The visitor center features an exhibit called "All the World is Watching Us: Little Rock and the 1957 Crisis." Large black-and-white photos on the walls give the history of the event. Although this is a small memorial, it is a powerful statement. In honor of the 50th anniversary, ground has been broken for a new visitor center.

At the Little Rock Nine Memorial, captions tell what happened to each student after their ordeal. All graduated and went on to college and successful careers.

Beals is an author and worked as a journalist for People magazine and NBC. Eckford served in the Army and as a journalist and became a social worker. Green, managing partner and vice president of Lehman Brothers in Washington, D.C., served as assistant secretary of housing and urban affairs under President Jimmy Carter. Gloria Karlmark, now retired, was a computer science writer and successfully published magazines in 39 countries. Terrence Roberts is a professor and clinical psychologist, and Trickey is a social worker and writer active in environmental causes.

On Feb. 23, federal supervision of the Little Rock district ceased. Although there has been progress, black students in Little Rock, as well as in the nation as a whole, on average score lower than white students on state and national standardized tests. The present administration of the district has resolved to continue assessing the students' progress.

The success of the Little Rock Nine, who were formerly denied an equal education, is an indication of how the practice of segregation not only robbed some students of a fair education but robbed our country of their talent.

Offbeat Travel

Museum Captures Lincoln's Spirit

Of the 15 presidential museums we have visited, Carla and I agree that the Abraham Lincoln Presidential Library & Museum in Springfield, Ill., is the most exciting and entertaining. Although a bit like one of the Orlando, Fla., attractions, it still remains true to the history of our country, making it very palatable to visitors.

We were left with two strong impressions. First, it was like walking into a Madame Tussaud's wax museum based on a single celebrity and the people in his life. Second, after watching their two major presentations our reaction was: "Wow, how did they do that?"

A dozen tableaus recapture scenes of important moments and people in President Abraham Lincoln's life. These full-size figures have a startling reality with their animated expressions and life-like eyes. We saw the young Lincoln lying in front of the fireplace embers teaching himself how to read as his snoring dog slept at his feet. He shared the one-room cabin with his father, stepmother and three stepsiblings.

Later we see the young lawyer in his office reading as his two young sons tear the place apart. Several of the characters from his life surprised me when I first recognized they were not fellow visitors, but were other life-like figures. John Wilkes Booth startled me the most. Also looking very hale and healthy were George McClellan, U.S. Grant, Sojourner Truth and Frederick Douglass.

The most disturbing tableau was that of a family of slaves on the auction block being separated by their new owners.

One room has a display of the dresses of the main ladies of society who were contending with Mary Lincoln for control of social leadership in Washington, D.C. The saddest of a number of scenes with her is the one where she sits in a depression after the death of her second son.

The "wow" experience came the first time when we watched "Ghosts of Lincoln." After an introduction to the museum from a big television screen in a large room, we thought we had seen the show when suddenly the doors opened to an even larger theater.

I should have guessed something unusual was to happen since a glass wall stood between the audience and the historian introducing us to the library. He said he would explain the ways in which historical material is collected and analyzed. During the presentation, smoke would appear and slowly take the form of Lincoln or others, and voices would speak. Once, smoke rose from one of his books and took form - sheer visual magic.

All of this did not prepare us for the final act when a wind began to blow a flag on the stage. The presenter stepped to a coat rack, put on a Union army jacket and began to tell us about his experiences in the War Between the States. The solid-looking library became a battlefield scene. As what now had to be an actor on film, he continued to talk to us as his body slowly disappeared and we were left with only his voice.

I still don't know if the actor was really there for the first half of the program or I had just seen one the best 3-D presentations ever. Later, in an even larger theater, we saw the multimedia presentation of "The Eyes of Lincoln."

At that performance I assumed the solid-looking man moving around on the stage telling us about major events in Lincoln's life was an illusion. This was confirmed as he moved back and forth between what appeared to be live action on the stage and action on the screen.

The same technique was used as we passed a series of windows with citizens giving their reactions to the Emancipation Proclamation. In the tableau in this room, each of Lincoln's Cabinet members has been faithfully reproduced so we could observe the room when he puts forward his intention to free the slaves. A man dressed as a secretary walked among the Cabinet members explaining how each of them was reacting. This figure was real. I touched him. The experience does leave the visitor with a question of what is reality.

The architect has been very generous with space. Besides the large theaters and the tableaus there are such rooms as the one with walls full of cartoons attacking Lincoln as a country bumpkin, a clown or a devil; and a separate presentation on questions asked by children with answers given in Lincoln's own words.

Part of what the museum tries to do is to take some of the myth out of Lincoln's life and show the real man who suffered, worked hard and questioned what he was doing.

Wayne P. Anderson

Kellogg Preached Virtues of Cereal and Evils of Sex

Visiting the Dr. John Harvey Kellogg Discovery Center, a small museum in a rebuilt Adventist Village in Battle Creek, Mich., was especially interesting to me. At the same time that Kellogg encouraged some very advanced health practices, he held some rigid Victorian sexual beliefs.

Kellogg is known today as the co-developer of corn and wheat flakes and for maintaining that these cereals were healthier for his patients than heavy breakfasts of fat and protein.

Shortly after the turn of the 20th century, however, he was better known as the director of the Adventist Battle Creek Sanitarium and Health Spa, which was established to promote holistic health.

Along with Ellen White, a brilliant thinker and religious leader of the time, he encouraged practices that were far in advance of the times, especially in diet, exercise, fresh air and sunshine.

Kellogg's patients read like a who's who of the 20th century: J.C. Penney, Montgomery Ward, George Bernard Shaw, Harvey Firestone, Thomas Edison and former President William Taft.

When he began as a doctor, medical practice consisted largely of bleeding, using calomel to purge the system and drugging patients with arsenic and mercury combinations. Indications are that it would have been common for patients to die of the cures in the late 1800s rather than of disease.

The doctors of the time felt that Kellogg's idea about diet as therapy was a foolish fad. They also felt night air was deadly, that sunshine was detrimental to your health and fresh vegetables were not good for you. Passersby who saw a man on a street corner eating three tomatoes assumed he was trying to commit suicide.

Patients at the sanitarium were allowed no alcohol, tobacco, caffeine, sugar, meat or hot spices. Instead they were given fresh fruit and vegetables and grains. Kellogg was one of the first

Americans to recognize the potential of processed soy to serve as a meat substitute.

On display at the museum are the machines he invented to measure strength, provide exercise and stimulate the body.

The machines are in working condition so that the visitor can use them to get an idea of the healthy behavior being encouraged. There was a saddle on a bucking machine, arm and leg exercisers that could be sold today as miracle reducing devices, vibrating machines to stimulate your feet and lower legs and mysterious electrical machines and lights to stimulate the bare body. Hydrotherapy was also used.

Despite his many modern ideas about health, he believed most of the Victorian ideas about the horrors of sex. As I point out to my Human Sexuality class at the University of Missouri-Columbia, Kellogg had some not-so-advanced ideas about the bad effects of an active sex life. He wrote a book that is loaded with myths about the terrible effects of masturbation, birth control and too-frequent intercourse.

A fact that is not mentioned either at this museum or at Kellogg's Cereal City USA is his campaign to control human sexual behavior. He believed that eating meat increased an individual's sexual desires and that substitute foods needed to be found to lower the sex drive. In his thinking, corn flakes fulfilled that goal.

The version of corn flakes he sold was for medicinal purposes and available only if you were a patient at the sanitarium or could order it by mail. He had no desire to make it a readily available commercial product.

His brother William felt the product had great commercial possibilities. He improved the flavor with the forbidden sugar and broke away from John to build the Kellogg's cereal manufacturing plant

Besides the visit to the museum, I also took a tour of the Adventist Village that attempts to capture the lifestyle of the early days of the church in the middle of the 19th century.

The Adventists were famous at that time for their active support of the Underground Railroad that rescued slaves from the South and transported them to freedom in Canada.

The young college men who led the tour were knowledgeable, friendly and obviously dedicated to the church.

Offbeat Travel

Elgin Marbles Still Vex British-Greek Relations

In the fifth century, Greek artists under the direction of Phidias sculpted 176 yards of a frieze for the famous Parthenon. The marble frieze decorated with resting gods, horsemen, athletic young men, chariots and warring centaurs ran around the entire top of the sacred shrine.

In 1801 the sculptures were thought by the British to be in danger of being destroyed. According to the British, Lord Elgin rescued them and brought them to the British Museum. Elgin, after whom the marbles are named, says he had permission; the Greeks say he didn't.

Years ago when we visited Athens, the Greeks' point of view was that Elgin had stolen them and that the only honorable thing for Britain to do would be to return them. When we visited the Parthenon, the few remaining carved blocks were covered with soot and not very striking. It was easy to believe Elgin had done the art works a favor by taking them to a secure protected spot inside the British Museum.

Some years later in London, I found the British attitude was that without their intervention there would be no sculptures for anyone to see. The Greeks were just too careless, and did I know that they actually used the Parthenon as a munitions dump? What if the Turks had sent a shell into it? And besides, London had more visitors, so more people would have an opportunity to appreciate them.

On my most recent trip to London, I stopped by to visit the 56 large panels that Lord Elgin chiseled off the frieze of the Parthenon and the 17 figures he threw in as an extra bonus for his good work. They are in large accommodations just back from the room with the Rosetta Stone, which the French took from the Egyptians and the British took from the French. It is apparent that the British Museum probably has more stuff liberated from other countries than any other museum in the world.

Museum staffs in Italy and Spain emphasize how much stuff they have that indicates their history. The British Museum staff is rightly proud of how much stuff they have that tells the story of the history of the world. In March I was there on a weekday, and the museum was overrun with tourists, groups of school children and locals soaking in the ambience of one of the world's finest collections of antiquities.

But the Greeks haven't given up. Before the 2004 Olympics they attempted to get the marbles on loan and even promised to build a special museum just to display them. They trotted out the marbles that had been left to them and showed how they are now in better shape, because they have cleaned with lasers, than the ones in Britain that had been cleaned with steel brushes.

Their publicity must have been good, because a BBC poll of the British public found that they were overwhelmingly in favor of returning them. The director of one of the other major British museums, the Victoria and Albert, suggested loaning them on a permanent basis, but the director of the British Museum has said, "No way."

Personally I think returning them could be a disaster for the British Museum. Everyone worries about the famous slippery slope. Give on one point, and you will be expected to give on another and another until you have nothing left.

Give the Elgin Marbles back to Greece, and the Egyptians will want the Rosetta Stone back, and soon everybody else will want to get in on the action.

Better they should be left where 5 million visitors a year can see for free some of the most interesting items in world history.

Part of the controversial Elgin Marbles

Wayne P. Anderson

Exploring India's 'Caves'

The Caves of Ajanta in India are in a horseshoe-shaped valley where 29 Buddhist temples, shrines and monasteries were carved out of the stone cliffs between 200 B.C. and 700 A.D.

In my mid-50s, I spent six weeks riding the trains with a British travel group in India and seeing most of the major sights, among them the ancient Caves of Ellora and Ajanta. Both are UNESCO World Heritage Sites, worth your attention if you find yourself between Bombay and Agra.

Although I will continue to use the designation "cave," the use of the word is misleading because these structures, some three stories high, are hand-carved out of rock. They are temples, shrines and monasteries and are filled with religious carvings, statues and paintings.

One of my journal entries reads:

"I'm surprised at how light I'm learning to travel. The clothes on my back, razor, toothbrush, soap, towel, sheet, camera and medicine, a book to read and my notebook. Oh yes, a small water jug. On this trip I didn't need the sheet or the towels. One can travel here for four or five days with just stuff in your pockets." Actually, traveling light was a necessity since my checked suitcase did not reach me until I was ready to leave the country.

"We caught a bus to Ellora Caves and spent the rest of the day exploring them. Getting on the bus when it arrived was certainly a mad rush - one had to forget one's gentlemanly impulses if you're to compete for seats. Many people stood for much of the four-hour trip."

I found the Caves of Ellora impressive. They are hewn out of solid stone, with large hallways and intricate carvings and pillars. They are in three groups, 12 Buddhist, 17 Hindu and five Jain. Even if modern tools and explosives had been available, these would still have been tremendous undertakings. It is hard to image making monuments of this size with only the hand tools available 350 to 700 A.D., when they were carved out.

To me the most impressive was No. 16, a Hindu temple that took 100 years to chisel out of the stone and has columns three stories high. It is twice the size of the Parthenon in Athens and is filled with statues of a variety of gods.

My journal the next day says:

"Well, here I am in Ajanta. I've really lucked out in getting to see both these and the Ellora Caves. ... This is a remarkable setting; we're in a horseshoe-shaped valley, and the caves are along the base of the horseshoe. The 29 caves at Ajanta are older than those at Ellora, having been carved out of the cliffs between 200 B.C. to 700 A.D. These caves are exclusively Buddhist, and as a result the stories painted on the walls were more interesting to me than the Hindu works in Ellora."

The caves had been lived in until 650 A.D. by Buddhist monks, scholars and students. When rediscovered by the British in 1819, they were clogged with debris.

"Each of the major caves had a man assigned - who was supposed to guide visitors for no tips, but the guides tend to ignore the Indian visitors and focus on foreigners and really work you for a tip. Less than one rupee seems unacceptable."

Some caves were quite dark, and in some, the guide could direct sunlight off a reflector to highlight objects. Things have improved, and visitors today can purchase a lighting ticket, which when presented to the guard has him turn on the lights so the paintings can be seen.

Rocks were a big thing at Ajanta. Salesmen were all over, aggressively selling various unique rock forms. I'm sure the rocks were valuable, but I wasn't about to carry rocks home. The last guide at Cave 24 produced one for me cheap - he wanted only 10 rupees. As I turned to go, he dropped the price immediately to one rupee. I had a terrible time convincing him I didn't want it even at that price.

Was a Black Lawman the Real Lone Ranger?
WAYNE AND CARLA ANDERSON

FORT SMITH, Ark. - That the likely model for the Lone Ranger was Bass Reeves - an ex-slave who worked most of his career as a deputy U.S. marshal for a famed hanging judge - was one of the most interesting things we learned when we visited here.

A tour of Fort Smith National Historic Site in Fort Smith, Ark., includes a stop at the gallows, where 79 men were hanged. Visitors can also see the old courthouse and exhibits on U.S. marshals who helped bring order to the West. The area was a national control point for the relocation of American Indians to what is now Oklahoma.

We attended a lecture by Art Burton, a black historian from Chicago who has spent much time in the Arkansas-Oklahoma area studying blacks' contributions to the settling of the West. Among his three books on this era is a biography of Reeves, whom he indicated was probably the greatest law enforcement officer to bring order to the West.

Reeves arrested thousands of criminals, could shoot straighter, lift more and do things that only movie heroes ordinarily can do.

He was black, therefore the mask; he was a master of disguise, which he often used to penetrate areas where criminals were. He had a lot of similarities to the Hollywood Lone Ranger, his American Indian friend, Tonto, and his horse named Silver. Reeves had lived with American Indians, spoke their language and often rode with one as a companion. He gave out silver dollars and among the many horses he used was a large white stallion.

Why the connection between Reeves and the Long Ranger? Many of the criminals arrested by him were sent to prison in Detroit, the city where the concept of the Lone Ranger was developed.

When Burton first heard the stories about Reeves, he thought they were legends because his exploits seemed so impossible. Careful research on his part showed that the legends were for the most part true.

Burton thought Fort Smith was one of the most important, if not the most important, of the historic towns in the West.

After lunch at Rolando's, a favorite restaurant among the residents of Fort Smith, we walked over to the Fort Smith National Historic Site, run by the National Park Service. As is usual when the NPS is involved, this was a first-class operation.

Our tour started with a 23-minute film on the history of Fort Smith. We learned that this had been an important national control point because American Indian tribes passed through here as they were being moved to Indian Territory, now Oklahoma.

American Indian police were in charge of controlling crime among American Indians but were not allowed to arrest whites. For a time, deputy U.S. marshals were not allowed into Indian Territory. As a result, a large number of criminals hung out in safety there. To help bring law into Arkansas and Indian Territory, President Ulysses Grant sent in Judge Isaac Parker, who became known as the "hanging judge" because of the large number of prisoners he sentenced to the gallows.

The original prison was in the basement of the courthouse, which was part of the old fort that had stood here. In the open prison area, many men were crowded together under primitive and horrific conditions. As we stood in the center of the area, voices came from speakers in different parts of the ceiling, re-enacting and explaining events that had happened here.

The second floor of the fort has the main exhibits, which are a combination of large posters with information about different groups from the area, glass cases with weapons and tools of the time, cells like those built when the prison was moved to this floor and interactive videos on the Indian Territory, the Trail of Tears and preserving American Indian and pioneer culture. These videos include commentary from present-day descendants of the early period and demonstrations of aspects of American Indian culture, such as dance.

We found the most informative presentation to be a film on the deputy U.S. marshals who were sent in to help Parker bring law and order to the area. These deputies were paid little, took great risks and had an unusually high death rate. The film said that 100 of them were killed carrying out their duties. This is higher than the number of murderers who were hanged at Fort Smith. Of the 150 men sentenced to hanging, only 79 met the hangman.

Parker never attended a hanging, and the hangman was not paid extra for his services. At a reconstruction of the original gallows near the courthouse, a recording describes what went on here.

Fort Smith is one of those places rich in historical events. The town struck us as having the richness of history that we find in St Joseph or Independence.

Museum Scrapes Away Mysteries of Dentistry

Did you ever wonder about the origin of the expression "4F," meaning unfit for military service? That's one of the interesting things I learned while visiting the Sindecuse Museum of Dentistry at the University of Michigan in Ann Arbor.

The main exhibition starts with dentistry during the Civil War, when extraction of bad teeth was the main procedure and was often performed by non-dentists. The Confederacy established a professional dental group whose main job was extractions. As many men had poor teeth, a rule was established that a man must have four front incisors that matched to enable him to tear open the cardboard cartridge for his rifle. If he did not, he was called "4F," a term that expanded to become the term for those who did not meet the minimum standards for service.

Dentists brought their own tools to the Army, and the tools were considered so precious they were considered military equipment. Gold foil was used for fillings for people with money and tinfoil for those with less.

The museum, in the large new dental school on the main campus, is not large but gives an interesting overview of the history and present state of the profession. Because I had recently had some serious dental work done, I was especially interested in finding out what the processes would have been like in earlier years.

When the U.S. Army formed a dental corps in 1911, dentists automatically became first lieutenants. Their instruments, along with rifles and machineguns, were considered tools of war. A foot pump that drove the dental drill had been invented. To save the energy of the dentist, the soldier who was to have work done had to come an hour early to provide the foot power for the drill used on the patient right before him.

Examples of dental offices on display are the pre-electric office of 1880, the early electric office of 1900 and the more up-to-date office of 1940. One section shows the development and problems of the use of tooth X-rays. The dentist had to adjust the intensity of the rays by looking at the bones of his hand on the machine. Not knowing the dangers of the rays led to serious burns and early deaths from cancer. Another section discusses the stages of development of dentistry with children.

The museum has more than 10,000 items showing the changes in dental technology from the late 1700s through the 1960s. Several projects are ongoing, and officials are searching for donations of 19th century equipment and dental supplier catalogs dating from 1940 to 1970.

Given what I saw about advances in dentistry, I can understand why when I was a child, many people older than 50 had lost all their teeth and why many of us older people today still have a full mouth of teeth.

Section 3

For Real Novelty Visit Any of the Following

Offbeat Travel

Would-be Actors Make Ends Meet on the Street
CARLA and WAYNE ANDERSON

We have found service in restaurants in the Los Angeles area to be excellent as actors waiting to be discovered ply this trade with extra flourishes, never knowing which customers might have the right connections.

So what do unemployed actors in Hollywood do besides work as waiters and waitresses? Our visits to the Los Angeles area have given us some insights into this burning question.

Costumed Superheroes

If the actor has the proper heroic build or looks like George Clooney or Christopher Reeves, he can get a superhero costume and work the crowds on Hollywood Boulevard outside Grauman's Chinese Theatre.

On a visit to see our daughter Debra, we spent a day enjoying the sights and sounds of what appears to be the newly renovated tourist section of the boulevard.

Clustered in front of Grauman's were Superman, Batman, Captain America and Wonder Woman. Further down the street was Spiderman.

He is the hero of our three-year-old twin granddaughters. Molly's favorite thing is to dress up as Spiderman and race her battery-propelled motorcycle around the house. Kate frequently borrows the outfit and the motorcycle; although she even more often cycles around the house with her princess dress billowing out behind her.

What a photo op this was for Grandma Carla and Aunt Deb, who could score points by having a picture taken as evidence they had met Spiderman and pretended to share in one of his adventures.

These actors are paid solely by the tips tourists give them for posing with them. They put in long days and often lunch together at a small local café. We hear if you drop in, you might see Elvis eating with Superman or Marilyn sharing a table with Frankenstein.

My wife and daughter meet Spiderman

Small Theaters

The play scene in Los Angeles is unusual, with no section of town similar to London or New York where you can find a wide choice of live theater. We had expected that as the Mecca for actors - many who would be out of work - that there would be such a surplus of talent that live theater would do well.

When we have been there, we have usually found one or two major productions, usually road shows such as "The Lion King," but for anything else, we have to hunt. We did once catch Jason Alexander (George on "Seinfeld") between television seasons on stage in a pleasant comedy. Mostly, however, what we have found are small theaters that can best be described as ratty.

The actors have been virtual unknowns whose credits are mostly small parts on television. The last show we went to had 50 seats, of which 18 were filled. The furniture on the stage was early Salvation Army, but the script called for the actors to comment on how classy it was.

The play "Sylvia" was about a man whose dog could talk to him. The dog, played by an attractive young lady, takes over his entire life and introduces him to the beauties of the outdoors and gets other people with dogs talking to him expanding his friendships. The downside was that he lost his job and his marriage began to crumble.

We also saw "Across 2," an excellent two-character play in Santa Monica that had a full house of 50 people. One of its drawing points was that there were two casts who played on alternate nights so that the audience could come back and see a different interpretation of the play.

On a previous trip we saw a play about Minnesota Scandinavians that was in the vein of "How to Speak Minnesotan."

Wayne talked with the stage manager after the show; he said it had been a real problem finding actors who could do a Swedish or Norwegian accent. After a good beginning, they would all fall back on the easier Irish accent.

The final cast members were all originally from Minnesota, where the accent is part of one's inheritance.

Unemployed or underemployed, we did notice that the typical person on the streets of Los Angeles was above average in looking physically fit and attractive.

Wayne P. Anderson

Trials at Old Bailey Are Lessons in Law and Order

When I lived in London, one of my favorite pastimes was watching the trials at Old Bailey. Especially for fans of our current "Law & Order"-type television programs, English trials provide an interesting contrast to American procedures.

The Old Bailey - a prominent building not far from St. Paul's Church - was once the Newgate Prison that figures so prominently in Charles Dickens' work. The trials held there are open to the public, and the guards will indicate where the most interesting cases are in session. These are likely to be murder or rape cases.

On one of my visits, another old guy who was a regular came up to me and asked how such and such a trial had come out. He'd seen me every time I'd been there and assumed I was a regular. Obviously a group of trial aficionados keeps track of the outcomes of the longer trials for one another.

The judge and the barristers, known here as trial lawyers, in their wigs and robes, are polite to one another. On one of my first visits I watched a murder trial. The defense barrister was doing the questioning, but if I hadn't known, I would have said he was the prosecutor.

The young man had evidently killed his father in an argument, then had phoned the authorities as if he were a neighbor and had come back after the police arrived. Later he said he had found his father dead and had panicked. The more he talked, the more he sounded guilty.

The question I had was why his lawyer didn't help him get his story straight before he put him on the stand. At that point, I was just beginning to understand that an English barrister doesn't see his job as getting his client off at any cost but instead as just ensuring that he gets proper representation.

Later, when I was introduced to a barrister, I told her I found it hard in following the line of questioning of the witnesses to tell the prosecution from the defense.

She said, "Why should you?" I explained that in America the defense usually worked out the story with the defendant, did a lot of objecting to the prosecution's evidence and questions, and, all in all, did everything possible to get the defendant off.

In a tone indicating that I was not too bright, she explained that a trial was a way of discovering the truth and that was the main reason for having a trial. She said any collusion between the barrister and the accused would get in the way of that goal. As an American, I found that a rather novel approach.

In America, witnesses have often been carefully rehearsed. At least they have gone over their testimony with someone so that they don't keep contradicting themselves or continue to say they don't remember.

One day when I had a female visitor with me, the guard at the door suggested that the trial in progress was not a good one to watch because it involved homosexuality, what they call buggery.

The Brits are evidently very sensitive about this subject because the jury was not only all-male but also all older males, as opposed to the murder trial we watched next, which had a jury that seemed quite young and included seven women.

In the first trial a young man had brought a rape charge against two other males, but as the lawyers politely worked him over it looked like a made-up story to protect himself against his mother's anger at his homosexual activities. Part of the problem was that he changed what happened too often. They had tied him to a chair; no they had tied him to a table turned upside down on a bed. The female barrister seemed very friendly to him and led him around without his seeming to have any awareness of how inconsistent he was being.

The murder trial involved a barroom brawl in which one man had been stabbed to death before a rather large number of witnesses, four of whom testified during the time we watched.

I had watched trials of barroom murder before and noticed an interesting phenomenon.

In being certified, the witness would be asked how many years he had been coming to that pub and how much he had drunk that evening. Usually the witness was a regular who had been frequenting that pub for many years.

The remarkable thing to me was the number of drinks - usually five to seven pints - that had been drunk before the incident. The barrister would then say, "You were quite sober then?" and the witness would reply, "Yes, I was."

Personally, five to seven pints of their beer would have put me in another realm of reality.

One morning, it took me awhile to find something to watch because many of the trials were just getting started. I found a plea situation with no jury. The young man had killed his mother because she had spoiled his dinner. She had not wanted to take him home from the mental hospital and was trying to find some other place for him to live. He made mouth movements and jerked his leg as he listened to the psychiatrist's testimony and smiled when the judge sentenced him to a mental hospital for treatment. He was the first accused I'd seen who was dressed up with a tie and a new haircut.

Friends and relatives visiting me from the United States often found observing trials at the Old Bailey one of the high points of their trips.

Offbeat Travel

Gumshoes and Trick Shoes: Spy Museum Amuses

WASHINGTON, D.C. - When I visited the International Spy Museum in Washington, D.C., I found it a highly interactive and entertaining experience, which included examining the largest public collection of espionage artifacts that were actually used.

The adventure began when, from a number of choices, I picked up an undercover persona and memorized details about that person's life. My cover was as a 56-year-old Brazilian carpenter on his way to Lisbon on family business. Soon I had to pass a test on my cover before being given instructions for the mission I would be tested on later. Next I was off to the briefing room to view a movie on the motivations, tools and techniques of real-life spies. In the "School for Spies" section, interactive exhibits tested my powers of observation and analysis - my ability to recognize threats to my cover, spot surveillance devices and drop boxes, and recognize someone I had seen before who was now in disguise. As an avid reader of mysteries, I felt I had done very well on those tests.

Alas, so much happened on my way to the final test, more than three hours later, that I found I had completely forgotten who my contact was and some details of my assignment. I was humbled when I blew the final test.

Many of the objects on display went back to World War II and the Cold War, some of the more interesting being a lipstick pistol, a cyanide gas gun that had actually been used to kill two people, a coat with a buttonhole camera and some explosive coal to be deposited in a factory boiler. I saw examples of dozens of listening devices and bugs, and at one interactive station I could listen on three bugs that had been placed in separate places in the museum.

Miniature cameras were on display, and much miniaturization had been accomplished before the more recent advances in computer chips. One of the most interesting cameras was one attached to the breast of a pigeon that would fly over enemy installations and take pictures on its way back to its station. One room was given over to the early use of pigeons carrying messages.

One of the more amusing devices was a transmitter that could be placed in the heel of the target's shoe, who would then become a walking radio station transmitting his conversations to a nearby monitoring post.

Throughout the exhibits there were interesting films, some from OSS files of World War II, others of later events such as the Sen. Joseph McCarthy hearings and the search for spies in the government. One film explained how two women agents had broken Aldrich Ames' cover. Ames, a member of our security, had been in the pay of Russians for many years and had given up 30 of our agents. A special room focused on Berlin during the Cold War because it had the heaviest concentration of spies in history. At one point, it was noted that that title has probably passed on to Washington, D.C.

A museum section on the history of spying started with the Bible. President George Washington was big on collecting information from his agents, and Daniel Defoe, author of "Robinson Crusoe," was the father of the British Secret Service. Ian Fleming, the author of James Bond stories, had been an intelligence agent.

A section on coding focused on the Navajo codetalkers - a code that was never broken. Also on display was an original Enigma cipher machine used by the Germans in World War II. An exhibit mentioned the mental brilliance of the Allied cryptanalysts who broke that code. Efforts at code-breaking not only shortened the war but helped lead to the development of the computer.

For those who want even more interaction, the museum offered Operation Spy, an immersive experience in which the participants take on the role of U.S. intelligence officers trying to find a missing nuclear device before it falls into enemy hands.

The museum is a fun experience, with many items that you won't see anywhere else and a collection of films that gives a good history of what the real spy business has been and is like.

The executive director of the museum worked for the Central Intelligence Agency for 36 years, and his advisory board includes four former CIA operatives and a retired KGB general.

This Washington, D.C., museum had the longest lines of visitors eager to enter when we visited in August.

Wayne P. Anderson

The Sheik's Revenge

Before one of my trips to the Los Angeles area, I had heard a story about a sheik from Saudi Arabia who had burned down his luxurious house in Beverly Hills to spite his neighbors. One version said that after complaints from his Beverly Hills neighbors about the pornographic statues in his yard and his generally bad taste, when his house burned down he had let the lot go to weeds and left it as a community eyesore.

Beverly Hills is a plush and carefully cared-for area of Los Angeles. Good taste is important, even if it is sometimes a little ostentatious. Leaving a weed-grown lot is not consistent with the Beverly Hills image.

I always find Los Angeles exciting, and when I had a daughter living there, I visited once a year. If you have wheels to get around, you can find considerable amusement. The area not only has the famous movie and TV studios but also great museums and other entertainment.

In June, having time on my hands to explore, I took a tour in an old Cadillac hearse of the places where famous Hollywood personalities overdosed, committed suicide or were murdered. When we reached Beverly Hills I asked our driver if he could drive us past the vacant lot. There it was, tall grass and weeds visible through the gates and over the short wall, sitting alongside homes that cost many millions of dollars.

The driver's story was different from the one I had heard, so I went looking in the Los Angeles Times archives to see if I could find the real story.

The inside headline of the Times January 3, 1980, read, "Fire at Sheik's Mansion Evokes Little Sympathy." It appeared that neither his neighbors nor the general public were sympathetic to his loss. One story I heard said the neighbors stood on the streets watching it burn, drinking champagne and laughing. The Times quoted a neighbor as saying, "We're kind of happy about the fire. We hated what he'd done to the place—we think it was very, very ugly." Part of the ugly was plastic flowers (in Beverly Hills?) that he put in plastic flowerpots all around the walls.

The 38-room, $7 million home (1980 dollars) was gutted by the fire that broke out on a Tuesday night and continued to burn until Wednesday.

Who did it? The first speculation was that it was someone outraged by the sheik's taste in decoration. The fire, however, didn't do in the controversial nude statues—intimate parts of which the sheik had had gaudily painted in anatomically accurate detail. There was even speculation that the sheik had had it done since he had pulled the security guards the week before. At one time, our guide said there were as many as 200 suspects.

About a year later, the sheik's chauffeur was arrested. The police said the fire that had broken out on two floors had been set by a skilled arsonist. The fire had been set to cover up the theft of $500,000 in art objects. Our driver said the objects had been placed in plastic bags and hidden in the water under a bridge until such time as the thief thought the coast was clear and they could be put on the market.

I'm still not clear why the lot is being allowed to continue as an eyesore, especially in a neighborhood where at least one of the homes is worth $30,000,000. Maybe Saudi sheiks have long memories for neighbors who lack their artistic sensibilities.

Wayne P. Anderson

Small in Stature, Big in History: The *Santa Maria*

COLUMBUS, Ohio - Ten volunteers dressed as sailors and pirates crowded with us 14 tourists on the deck of the *Santa Maria* in Columbus. Our guide told us that the 1492 crew had included 39 seasoned sailors plus some teenagers in training. How in the world did they go about their duties without constantly bumping into each other on this small ship?

The pirates were actually out of place on the *Santa Maria* because it sailed long before they became a force in the world. But evidently the volunteers sometimes preferred re-enacting pirate times.

In 1992, for the 500th anniversary of the discovery of America, a group of Columbus businessmen had an exact replica of Christopher Columbus's *Santa Maria* built and anchored in the Scioto River in Columbus. Although they spent more than $1 million to have it constructed, they didn't plan for its upkeep, so finding money to keep it afloat as a tourist attraction has been difficult.

The 45-minute-plus tour was led by a woman well-informed about Columbus and life aboard ship. She was aided in telling the story by costumed volunteers covering such topics as cooking on board, the use of weapons and the mistaken ideas Columbus and his crew had of where they were.

The cook was stirring beans and salt pork over a charcoal fire. I suspect the original crew ate lentils because beans had yet to enter the European diet. The hard tack was said to have little food value but expanded to give a full feeling when moistened. The kegs of water began to go bad after a short time, and wine was added to improve the flavor. What they didn't know then was that wine not only covered the bad taste, the alcohol also killed some of the bacteria.

Costumed volunteers offer a view of what life was like aboard the *Santa Maria*.

Down times on the ship were filled with games. Board games such as chess were popular, as were card games. Rats were a problem because the food supply was kept below deck in the dark. A large wooden trap had been invented, and the rats were put in a box that dragged behind the ship until they drowned.

Small ledges on the outside of the deck were the toilets. Hanging your bottom out over the ocean looked dangerous to me. A cord with a brush on the end served as toilet paper.

At 98 feet in length, the *Santa Maria* was the largest of Columbus' three vessels, but I was still impressed with how small this ship was. We were told it was a "nao," or cargo ship, and not very good for exploration. This was proved when it ran aground on

Christmas Day in 1492 on what is now Haiti. It was taken apart for its timbers, which were used to build a fortress.

The replica ship lies across the river from the COSI, Columbus' major science museum, and this adds to the number of people who visit the *Santa Maria*. The ship is also within walking distance to the state Capitol. Groups of 30 or more can make arrangements to stay the night and experience more directly what life was like aboard. The next time you are traveling near Columbus, it's worth a stop. An attraction like this can bring alive a sense of history.

Offbeat Travel

The Rebirth of Unclaimed Baggage

The sign at the jewelry counter said, "Lady's diamond tennis bracelet, appraised value, $28,528, our price, $14,262." And hand-painted oriental silk robes were marked $1,000 each.

My youngest daughter and I were walking through the Unclaimed Baggage Center in Scottsboro, Ala., a small town within a 90-minute drive of her home in Chattanooga, Tenn. Here is where unclaimed luggage ends up when its owners can't be tracked down.

As we walked through the aisles of women's and men's clothes in the block-long building, I found a cashmere sport coat that would have looked good on me if the arms had been a little longer. The price? Just $65. The clothes had been newly cleaned, and some of the pieces were brand new. The owners probably bought them for that special vacation. The new-looking wedding gowns meant that someone's mementos of that special day had disappeared or maybe hadn't even shown up for the wedding. I did learn that travelers whose bags are lost at the beginning of a honeymoon or vacation are usually offered $500 by the airline to purchase what is needed so that their trip is not ruined.

We were also surprised to see wheelchairs, stacks of cameras, skiing equipment and baby strollers.

"I see everything but the kitchen sink," I told my daughter.

About 10 minutes later, my daughter said, "Dad, I've found the kitchen sink; it's in the unclaimed cargo section."

She went on to the baby-clothes section, where she bought half a dozen new outfits for her twin babies.

A staff member at the Unclaimed Baggage Center noted that, although only .005 percent (five out of 100,000) of all bags checked at airlines are permanently lost, this still results in the store's receiving 7,000 new items a day. More than a million items pass through the store each year.

These items come from three main sources. First, there is luggage that gets lost when the destination bar code is torn off and there are no address tags on the outside and no identification on the inside. Second, there are carry-on bags that passengers leave in the overhead compartment. I suspect that's where the large number of cameras I saw came from. The third group is composed of unclaimed business-to-business cargo. This is where the kitchen sink came in, but the items I saw also included hardware, cosmetics, fine perfume and even a stack of oriental rugs.

The lost luggage is sent to a regional warehouse owned by the airlines. It is held at least 90 days as attempts are made to find the owners. The baggage is then declared unclaimed and auctioned off. My impression is that most of it is bought by the Unclaimed Baggage Center.

At one of the entrances are two maps, one of the United States and another of the world. Both are filled with pins indicating where visitors are from. Customers have come from every state in the union and most foreign countries. The center is probably worth a trip if you're in Atlanta, Memphis, Nashville, Birmingham or Huntsville. But then, I'm not a big shopper; people obviously do come quite a distance to look for bargains.

The store has some amenities: a play area for children, a Cups Espresso Café serving Starbucks Coffee and an information desk to answer visitors' questions, including questions on where to stay and what else to see in the area.

Some Suggestions

If your luggage is lost, airlines will pay you up to $1,250 per person for all bags on domestic flights and about $10 per pound on international flights. That means you don't really want to put anything very expensive in luggage. If you do, you should take out additional insurance.

I always carry my cameras and any medicines in my carry-on luggage, but I put the same identification on and in this bag as I do on the sent baggage. Be sure to keep all the information on your tags up to date. I'm a bit paranoid about my carry-on, so I always try to be one of the first to sit in my section so I can put my bag directly overhead or slightly in front of my seat.

At some hub airports, such as Miami International Airport, your baggage is more likely to get stolen than lost. Since so many bags look alike, the thief can claim misidentification of the bag. To counter this, I put colored ribbons on my luggage so that I can spot my bags as they come out of the shoot.

If your bag does not appear at the claim area, find the baggage agent on duty immediately. On occasion, I've found that my bags have arrived before I have and were in the agent's area for safekeeping. Don't leave the airport until all the paperwork has been filled out, and get a phone number for follow-up. In my travel experience, luggage that did not appear at the claim area has always found me.

My worst case of missing baggage was in India, where I was reunited with my luggage as I was leaving New Delhi after a six-week tour of the country. That I had taken my basics in a carry-on bag turned out to be a lifesaver.

Wayne P. Anderson

House-on-the-Rock, an Impressive Fortress

The House-on-the-Rock in Wisconsin incorporates rock and waterfalls into its structure.

Driving toward the House-on-the-Rock near Spring Green, Wis., I saw giant, wildly designed pots along the roadway. This set the tone for exploring a remarkable collection of rooms unlike anything to be found anywhere else in the world. Alex Jordan, a man who wanted solitude, built a retreat in a remote area around Deer Shelter Rock that half a million people now tour annually.

After starring in high school football and trying several enterprises, Jordan retreated to a rock outcropping that he used as a foundation and began to build a house incorporating the rock and its waterfalls. In the beginning, he did the work alone, carrying cement and other heavy supplies up a 75-foot ladder. The house grew like a plant gone wild, moving in one direction after another. He would build a room, not like it and tear it down to build another. Visiting the house, I couldn't believe he had any particular goal in mind — he just had an irresistible urge to build.

Offbeat Travel

Jordan didn't like to travel, and he didn't like to have his picture taken. At first, he didn't particularly want visitors to his home, but they kept coming to see this remarkable structure. In 1960, he finally decided if they were willing to pay 50 cents, they could tour the house. He used the money to build more rooms and buy more of the music-making machines that fascinated him. Visitors spread the word, and soon people were lining up to see what he was doing. Today, people come from all over the world to see this imaginative but somewhat weird achievement.

Visitors have four choices of how to see the house and its surrounding features. I took the basic house tour because I understood this alone would take three hours. A visitor's center gives a biography of Jordan and history of how the house developed, with examples of what you will see later, such as music-making machines playing piano, violins and horns. These will be playing music in the house. Also in the visitor's center are animals Jordan created for a giant carousal.

Fourteen rooms make up the original house. Oriental art exists along with stained glass and bronze statues. One area has a three-story bookcase filled with rare books. There are no regular floors — that is, you can't say it's a five-level house. Instead, visitors might shift by small steps or by a short stairwell from one floor into the next area. The most impressive room, the "Infinity Room," extends 218 feet over the Wyoming Valley and contains more than 3,000 small windows.

The sections I missed would have taken a full day, but I heard them highly recommended. Included are a typical 19th century Main Street and Streets of Yesterday. Although music boxes are in many rooms, a tour of the Music of Yesterday area contains probably the world's greatest collection of animated and automated music machines. More than 260 of his handcrafted animals are on display in the world's largest carousel.

During the Christmas season — Friday to Jan. 2 — the house is transformed into a Santa town, with more than 6,000 Santas of all sizes and types on display. If you are looking for something different, you might give this a try.

Section 4

Some Family Matters

Keeping a Travel Journal

For the past 30 years, I have kept journals of my trips. This has resulted in my having a drawer full of various sized notebooks that remind me of the details of some of the most interesting experiences of my life.

When I'm traveling, at least once a day, I write down my observations and record what has happened. This serves a number of purposes. When I travel, so much is going on around me that if I don't record it the same day by the next day, it is overpowered by new material and I forget it. Also, with all the new scenes and events, I often don't get a chance to process or make sense of what I have seen. It is only later in rereading my notes that I see patterns and can draw some conclusions about what I have observed.

Do you ever wonder where you took that picture or what it is a picture of? Your journal should be of help to you in figuring it out. Years later, you will find that you have forgotten many details of what was at the time a great adventure. The journal brings events back to life.

I used to use my notes when writing letters to my daughters and my brothers and sister. Now of course, I use my notes for the articles I write for the *Columbia Daily Tribune.*

People occasionally ask me questions about some aspect of a country. At this point in my life, at my age, I can get confused or misremember what exists in what country. Places and events tend to get messed into one big ball, and my journals help me separate what is where.

Recently a friend asked about something in Panama, a country I had spent a month in some years ago while visiting my brother Lester. In rereading my journal, I was entertained by my observations. What follows are some examples of the kind of things I record in my journals.

Stories

"The Colombians who work for the Salvation Army feel that to keep your brain working right you must have a stew made of fish heads at least once a week. When one of their lieutenants didn't get it, she became quite mentally disturbed and physically ill. After they arranged that she could make it for herself, she got well."

Observations

"Les and I walked through the streets of a slum in Panama City this afternoon. Les sees this as a dangerous place because people frequently get robbed here. To me, the people looked happy and quite healthy. The air was one of enjoying living here. Panamanians stood talking on the corner and greeting each other and gave the scene a sense of community. As I walk the streets in the U.S., I don't see as many smiles or as many direct looks at people, implying physical fitness and a sense of well being. Everywhere I see lovers, friends and people who are proud."

"There is a special Panamanian dog; it's small, thin, with large pointed ears and eyes that beg. They don't bark much and are plentiful. Besides the dogs in the yards of the small country shacks, there were many naked little kids."

"People drive fast here and move into spaces that hardly seem to exist. Lester drives just like the Panamanians but complains constantly about what they're doing just as he makes the same chancy moves."

"Les was telling me today why you can't use the local post offices to conduct local business. Evidently it can take six months for a local letter to be delivered. Instead, you hire someone to hand deliver letters."

Experiences

"On my morning run, a large black bird has been dive bombing me — I swear his wing tips touch my neck. One day, he is going to misjudge and we will both be in trouble. Les suggested that I run that area backward or wave a rope above my head. Both sound like too much trouble."

"So, here I sit in a small hotel room in what we were told is the best hotel in Boqueta. It's still raining; the room is damp, as is the hard bed. There is no radio or TV (my goodness). A stream runs by our door and under the restaurant. Tropical plants surround us. As you come into the area, it is usual to stop at an overlook and say something like, "This sure looks like Switzerland."

"I spent hours walking the streets of Colon while Les ran a meeting at the church. The open sewers running between the buildings added nothing to its charm. Boys playing soccer in the side streets seemed little concerned about their balls rolling into the sewers. They just kicked them out and went on playing noisily and happily."

I have noticed that many confirmed travelers get out their pen in the evening and jot down their impressions. Some people include photos or postcards, draw pictures, paste in maps and brochures. So on your next trip consider taking a notebook and pen and recording what you see and what happens to you. Years from now, you'll be happy you did.

Wayne P. Anderson

Close Quarters Test Family Ties

Back in 1967 when our children were young and my wife, Carla, and I were financially pinched, we still had a great desire to travel. The on-the-cheap way to show our four little girls the world was to live in a tent. When there were just the two older girls, we traveled around the eastern part of the United States camping close to Civil War battlefields and state parks. The girls traveled well and enjoyed the closeness of living in a 9-foot-by-9-foot tent.

When we returned to Missouri, we wanted to continue this rustic travel tradition. As soon as our fourth child was 18 months old, we made a tenting trip to visit the Branson area. At this time it had not yet become one of the country's favorite entertainment centers. There were only a couple of country shows in the area, but Silver Dollar City was open and the *Shepherd of the Hills* play was presented during the summer months in an outdoor theater.

The cast of characters for our tenting experience was Carla, the mother, four daughters (11, 9, 3 and 18 months) and me, the father.

This was before light modern tent material, so the tent was heavy canvas treated with water repellent, and it tended to drip water from its sides if you held your fingers against it. While it had been possible for four to make it a temporary home, six people were too many, and if one person turned over in the night everyone had to change position. Frankly, it was seriously overpopulated.

Then the rain came, making a wet tent with small leaks here and there where fingers had been pressed against the sides. There were puddles everywhere and a sloppy one right in front of the tent that was ankle-deep.

It rained off and on, but the skies remained dark and threatening making it too nasty to go off to do much sightseeing. That meant we spent much of the time that week hanging out in the tent. We played games, sang songs and generally tried to amuse each other.

A major problem was the toilets, which were some distance from the tent. I would try to get to them when the rain had temporarily stopped.

"Does anybody need to go to the bathroom?"

Heads shook no.

"Are you sure?"

Innocent expressions all around. "Yes, Daddy."

As I was working my way back through the tent flap, daughter No. 3 greeted me with, "Daddy, I need to go potty." It had begun to rain again. Water dripped off my back.

"OK. Anybody else?"

"No, Daddy."

As I handed the 3-year-old back through the tent flap, water still falling on my back, I heard, "Dad, I think I need to go."

"OK. Are the rest of you sure you don't need to go?"

"I'm fine." The oldest said.

"Well, OK then, let's go."

The rain had turned to a heavy mist; it was difficult to avoid the puddles. My feet were beginning to squish in my shoes.

The relay of kids to the toilet area continued during the time we remained. No one's schedule matched that of the others. It finally occurred to me that this was one of the techniques the girls had developed to break the boredom of living in a tent under adverse conditions.

We did get out to see several plays, Silver Dollar City and the major cave in the area, but too much time had to be spent in close quarters. Even with a good-natured wife and well-behaved children, tensions built. After that week in a tent, Carla and I swore that we would never again travel with these children with a tent as our shelter.

The next summer we went shopping for a travel trailer and a station wagon to tow it. It had bunks for six, electric and gaslights, a gas stove, a shower, a refrigerator and, best of all, an indoor toilet.

Offbeat Travel

Life on an English Estate Wasn't Entirely Romantic

When I was teaching for the Air Force in Europe, the second place we lived in England was on an estate in Suffolk near the North Sea. Although I don't believe the owner had a title, he was considered a gentleman and was fairly high up in the English caste system. His family was definitely upstairs in the upstairs-downstairs system. For example, he shot pheasants with those who did have titles, and he had his own gamekeeper.

The gamekeeper was a silent, respectful man who knew his place in the English scheme of things and was managing to raise a large family. He appeared to feed his family on game from the estate, mostly rabbits. Like many working men in England, he always dressed in an ill-fitting wool suit jacket.

The wealthy landowners needed a gamekeeper because pheasant hunting in England is a ritual all of its own. The gentlemen shooters station themselves along an open field, each with his dog and a shotgun. Some even had a cane-like device with a small seat upon which they could sit as they waited for the pheasants to be driven toward them.

The gamekeepers and their families would start some distance from the shooters and, making noise, drive all game in the area toward them. As the pheasants rose into the air, a gun would bark, a pheasant would flutter to the ground, the shooter's dog would pick it up and a gamekeeper would place it in the waiting truck. A gentleman evidently never uses his legs when hunting if he can avoid it.

Hunters often "cured" the pheasants before eating them by hanging them in a cool area for a week or two. When they were properly ripe, they would be served for a special dinner. One holiday, Carla and I went to a fancy restaurant in Aldeburgh and ordered pheasant under glass. It tasted rotten. Later, the master of the estate told us that was what it was supposed to taste like after a proper hanging. He admitted he had never developed a taste for aged pheasant but that his father relished it.

On one of our first nights there, Carla and I were coming home through the estate with a light fog covering the road. In the darkness, we saw two small lights. We slowed and found we were passing a herd of deer who were quietly eating the tops off the carrots grown on the estate.

The house we lived in had been built sometime before Christopher Columbus landed in the New World. It adjoined the house of the gamekeeper and was set some distance from the home of the master of the estate. At one point, the king had taxed windows on the premise that only the wealthy could afford to own a home with large glass windows. As a result, the windows had been bricked in; only later were smaller ones put back in.

The oak trees on the land were also hundreds of years old and were hollow inside. Oak trees also had been taxed based on their value as lumber. The previous owners had topped them in such a way that they were no longer valuable as lumber but continued to grow and provided shelter for the deer.

The house was cold and hard to heat. In a move of economy, a pile of brick along the wall of the living room had been electrified so that they were warmed at night when the rates were low. They were then expected — falsely — to keep the house warm during the day. We were never able to convince our four daughters that it was in their best interests to come in and out of the house as quickly as possible. We would find them standing at the door talking to friends as the heat wafted out of the house.

They complained constantly about having to go to bed in frigid conditions because the upstairs area had no heat. We took to bringing an electric space heater into their room about 15 minutes before bedtime to take the worst of the chill from the air.

Men were shorter when the house was built; consequently, the door sills were low and set so that if I was hurrying to answer some emergency call from Carla, I was likely to strike my head. Given the primitive state of the kitchen and other facilities, these stress calls were quite frequent. My head bore the evidence in the form of a long scab in the middle of my forehead.

The children came up with a clever solution and at Christmas put sponge bumpers on all of the offending sills. After that I simply bounded off, eliminating the scars but leaving the headaches.

The water was hard, and washing one's hair in it left it feeling like straw. We considered ourselves blessed that there was a barrel of rainwater outside our door, and we availed ourselves of it to get soft, manageable hair. That is, until the day I came home to find the gamekeeper washing dead rabbits in it. It seemed this was a standard practice, and the water never seemed as attractive after that to the girls or me.

Wayne P. Anderson

Two Little Angels Make for a Hellacious Flight
WAYNE AND CARLA ANDERSON

My youngest daughter, Stephanie, was just back for her 20th-anniversary class reunion at Rock Bridge High School. If the reunion and visit home were a success, the flight to get here was a nightmare.

Stephanie has twin 2½-year-old daughters who have very different personalities. Typically they are fairly well behaved, so she assumed the flight would have its problems but she could manage.

They got to the airport in Chattanooga, Tenn., two hours early - as recommended - a real mistake with toddlers. With not enough to amuse them, they kept exploring the waiting area but in different directions.

Memo: Be sure to bring lots of new busy-work toys.

The Game's Afoot

One headed for a distant escalator, and Stephanie dropped her backpack and took off after her. With help from a passing lady, she caught the child, only to be informed by a ticket agent that she had just committed a misdemeanor by leaving behind her backpack. She would have committed a more serious misdemeanor of child endangerment had she not pursued the twin.

At this point, she considered aborting the trip and calling her husband to come and take her home.

Memo: Don't travel alone with two toddlers - have a backup chaser.

Changing planes in Memphis, Tenn., she mentioned at the ticket desk she needed help because the gate was so far away, and the person in charge politely said he would find help for her. Shortly before the flight was to leave, he had to inform her help was not available.

That meant a rush with a heavy backpack and two little girls with different attitudes toward the word "hurry." One ran off down the concourse, soon so far ahead people were wondering about the lost child. The other twin decided walking was as fast as she would go and refused to be carried. Fortunately, they made the last call for the flight to St. Louis.

Breaking the Rules

On the plane, the steward had given one of the women seated nearby a reprimand for not having her bag far enough under the seat, giving the impression this was to be an "obey all rules" flight. As the plane was waiting in line for takeoff, Stephanie's daughter threw a doll on the floor. Hoping not to be reprimanded for breaking rules, Stephanie quickly unclicked her belt, picked up the doll and re-clicked. This was so fast the man behind her was not aware anything had happened until the steward came up and said, "We are not leaving the runway if you can't keep your seat belt on. Do we need to make other arrangements for you?"

The seats of the twins were across the aisle from her, so she couldn't maintain the control over them she needed, and as a result, one twin kicked the seat in front of her and kept unlocking her seat belt. Memo: Insist on a seat between your toddlers.

When we met her at the airport, the children seemed to be perfect angels and ran eagerly forward to meet grandma and grandpa, but Stephanie was obviously stressed out. A physician, she is cool in emergency room situations and has a calming influence on mothers under stress. Flying with children, however, pushed her limits. She decided to return to Chattanooga in a rental car with grandma as a co-pilot.

Wayne P. Anderson

Bullfights!

Despite protests by animal-rights groups, bullfighting remains popular in many Spanish-speaking countries. If you travel in Spain, Mexico, Columbia, Venezuela, Peru and Ecuador, you will find bullrings. The best are probably in Madrid and Mexico City.

When we lived in Madrid some years ago, my wife, my four daughters and I decided to take in a bullfight. Dramatic posters of the toreros (bullfighters) leading the toros (bulls) in dangerous passes with their colored capes were everywhere. The excitement among the locals was the kind that we in Columbia reserve for a big football Saturday against Nebraska.

We had good seats halfway up in jam-packed Las Ventas Bullring late on a Sunday afternoon. What we saw was not sport in its usual sense, where both opponents have a relatively equal chance of winning. The odds were definitely on the torero. But from the start, we were in the presence of magnificent pageantry and drama. The bulls were fierce and eager, and the torero's gang of assistants in their tight, shiny suits were experts in annoying the bull.

At the start of a match, they would tease the bull with the cape to see which way he tossed his head and how he charged. Then a man on a horse used his spear to weaken the bull's shoulder muscles so that he would drop his head. Someone with beautiful moves planted two barbed sticks in the bull's back while the bull was charging him.

We didn't realize at the time how good the bullfighters were. It was only later that we could appreciate that we had seen the World Series of bullfighting, with only the best bulls and toreros in the country in the arena. Las Ventas was the Mecca for bullfighters.

Sometime later in Barcelona, Spain, having a free afternoon, we went to a bullfight at the Plaza de Toros Monumental. We should have stayed at home. It was definitely a day for amateurs.

First, some of toreros moved their feet as the bull charged. This indicated that the bull had made them nervous. None of them made their passes with the ballet-like moves of the toreros in Madrid, and the killings of the bulls were disasters.

After many boos from the audience, they would exchange the straight sword used for the cape passes for the slightly curved sword used for the kill. Those who were successful made three or four attempts to put the sword in the right place in the bull's neck to kill it. But some couldn't do it even then, and a big guy would come out from behind the barriers and hit the bull in the head with a special hammer.

This cured us of bullfights for some time.

Later, in Mexico City, we were told that there was to be a special corrida (bullfight) at the Lomas Bullring. A torero who had opened his career here years before and had become one of the foremost toreros in the country was making his final appearance before retirement.

I don't remember the other fights that day, but I do remember this man's last appearance in the ring. He was lucky to have drawn a fierce bull, because you can't impress the audience if the bull isn't brave.

After dominating the bull with pass after pass, he began to take unusual chances. He made passes while on his knees and went eyeball to eyeball with the bull. These moves were especially dangerous because the bull was learning and would soon know how to use his horns more expertly.

The audience went wild and began throwing flowers and other objects into the ring. When the torero finally made the kill, they awarded him with an armload of the bull's body parts. One ear is a special honor. He got both ears and the tail.

Bullfighting is a fact of life in these countries. I have no interest in traveling just to see a bullfight, but having seen some I feel I have made a closer connection with the people there.

Wayne P. Anderson

Bullfights Through the Eyes of a Child
By ROSIE ANDERSON HARPER

When my dad started talking about the bullfights we saw in Madrid, Spain, my reaction was, "That's not what I remember." Through the eyes of a child, the bullfight looked somewhat different.

First, I remember worrying about the bull. I grew up with the book "The Story of Ferdinand." All that bull wanted was to sit under the tree and smell the flowers. He did not want to fight the matador. What was going to happen to him? There was some, but not much, consolation when I found out the bull meat went to the orphanage after the slaughter.

My next strongest memory is the colorful parade of people strutting around the bullring. This was very different from the homecoming parade in downtown Columbia. The flashy sequined and mirrored costumes. The men in pants that came to the knee and jackets that did not come all the way to the waist. The matador with his gold ornate costume waving his red cape. The horses draped in festive scarves with their tails wrapped in ribbons. The anticipation of what was to come.

It was a strange mixture of violence and beauty. Being afraid of what I might see, I had brought a coloring book with me to hide behind if necessary.

The picadors rode in on horses and stabbed the back of the bull with long spears. The spears were wrapped in vividly colored ribbons of blue, red and yellow. The banderilleros came next and stabbed the bull with short, brightly colored spears. They seemed to keep at the bull for some time, and he ran around with the spears stuck in his back. This was the point where the coloring book held quite a fascination for me.

Luckily for the audience (but not for me), the bull did not act like Ferdinand, and he played the role well of being very angry and repeatedly charging the matador. I thought the smart people were the ones running behind the wooden barriers to get out of the bull's way.

The crowd loved the spectacle. There was loud screaming in a foreign language I did not understand. It was dusty, hot and crowded. I remember the people waving handkerchiefs, but can't remember what that signified. Their faces and bodies expressed excitement and joy. I don't think I quite "got it." My sister was bugging me and wouldn't leave me alone to hide behind my coloring book.

Finally, there came the part of the fight where the matador faced the bull alone in the ring. With a lot of fancy moves, the bullfighter waved the cape then stepped to the side of the charging bull just in time. It was just as my sister and I had pretended many times before, with one of us playing the matador and the other the bull. At some point, the matador got the killing sword and aimed for the bull's neck. He thrust the sword in several times and then it was over. The bull was dead.

The crowd went wild and threw many flowers to honor the bullfighter as he circled the ring. In the end, two horses unceremoniously entered the ring and dragged the bull out, leaving a long, bloody track in the sand.

I couldn't help but think of Ferdinand again. I thought the bull would have been much happier under a tree smelling the flowers. Come to think of it, I think I would have been happier if I could have joined him.

Wayne P. Anderson

Familiar Destination Hosts Travel Wonders

It never occurred to me that I would one day write a travel article on my hometown, Jamestown, N.D. After all, my goal was to escape those cold winters that keep the riffraff out.

That chill factor also motivates young people to get an education so they can flee to the warmer climes of Minneapolis.

Some years ago on a visit to give a series of lectures at my alma mater, Jamestown College, I was surprised to learn that as many as 175,000 visitors a year have stopped by to see the town's major sights: Frontier Village, a giant cement buffalo, a pasture with wild buffalo and the National Buffalo Museum.

Frontier Village is one of those sites that grows over the years and ends up being a significant attraction. Someone donated a railroad station from one of the defunct towns in the area.

Then a post office and jail were added, and a little later a one-room schoolhouse where a friend of mine taught in the 1930s and a small Lutheran church where another friend had been confirmed.

Soon came a fire department, saloon, barber shop, sheriff's office, trading post and an art studio and sales room a locally famous cowboy artist set up.

The operation was given a touch of class when fans of Western writer Louis L'Amour donated an old house where he might have lived. For those who aren't Western fans: Thirty of L'Amour's novels have been made into movies, and his books have been translated into 26 languages.

The original buildings were furnished just as they would have been in the early 1900s. Open from Memorial Day to Labor Day, local volunteers share stories about each building.

A place I was connected with as a child was a more recent addition. In the early 1930s, my dad used to take me on horseback - he didn't drive a car - over to the general store and post office in Eldridge, a small town about 12 miles from Jamestown.

Our big thrill was watching the train rush pass and seeing the crew throw out the incoming mail sack and hook the outgoing bag off the post-office hanger. After all that excitement, Pa would buy me a box of Cracker Jack with a special surprise inside. In those days, when a nickel was real money, the prizes were sturdy enough to last awhile, even in the hands of a 4-year-old.

When the dust storms blew away the crops, my family and many others were dispossessed. The eviction team moved our meager belongings out into the cool October countryside, including Ma's kitchen stove with bread baking in it. A local photographer came out and shot a picture of our sad-looking farm family, another set of victims of the Depression.

Ma was so embarrassed she destroyed her copy of the picture. Sixty years later, a copy was found among her sister Selma's belongings, and my brother, a minister who is also an artist, made a painting from it.

If you visit the Eldridge General Store and Post Office at Frontier Village, you will note the painting right at the entrance.

The 4-year-old with the smile is me; the 2-year-old with the frown is Lester, the artist. He seems more aware of the significance of what was happening than I was.

You can see the site from some distance down Highway 94 because it is near the "World's Largest Buffalo," a concrete monument 26 feet high, 46 feet long and weighing 60 tons.

Roaming in a large pasture next to Frontier Village and the concrete buffalo is a herd of 50 wild buffalo, including White Cloud, an albino that would have been considered sacred by the area's American Indians. For years, it was the only albino buffalo in existence, but I was told another had been born.

About 100 yards from Frontier Village is the National Buffalo Museum, open all year. The museum features artifacts and artwork of the Plains Indians and a video on the history of American bison.

Many visitors come in RVs and trailers, as there is a campground adjacent to the village. You can get buffalo burgers at the chuck-wagon restaurant above the gift shop there.

I realize North Dakota is one of the least visited states, but if you're passing through, it's worth taking a look at an important slice of prairie history.

My family gets moved off the farm in 1934.

Section 5

Getting Personal

Offbeat Travel

Fear of Flying

I have logged a lot of air miles during the past 46 years, but when I started, I had a real fear of flying.

In my early 30s, I had a realistic dream in which the plane I was flying in crashed. Ordinarily, I don't see dreams as prophecies, but this was coupled with a feeling that flying isn't really possible. After all, doesn't it seem unreasonable that you can be inside a heavy metal tube, 30,000 feet in the air, traveling at 550 miles an hour?

When I was 35, an occasion arose where I was supposed to be in Dallas one day and in Buffalo, N.Y., the next. Even with good bus or train connections, that's not possible. Decision time was at hand. Did I want to be safe and miss a lot of life's richness of experience? Or would I take a chance and fly?

Fly it was.

Initially — that is, for the first 10 years — I was a white-knuckled flyer to the max. I needed a couple shots of Scotch before boarding and whatever alcohol they would give me after I got on board. Each new noise, lurch or sudden dip would send adrenaline charging through my body. My heart would pause and my breathing stop.

Slowly, I learned more about what was happening. That noise on takeoff was the sound of the wheels coming up. Those changes in the whine of the engine were normal, and there were noises connected with preparations for landing. Turbulence was to be expected when crossing mountains. On occasion, I still stared at the bulkhead, wondering what the last moments would be like as the explosion from the terrorist bomb hurtled toward me.

The methods I used and taught clients to use for anxiety management simply didn't work for me when I got on an airplane.

When I began to feel less distressed, something would happen to restore my fears. On one trip to Europe, we were 90 minutes out over the Atlantic when the pilot said on the intercom in a reassuring voice, "We're having a minor problem with one of the engines and, just to be on the safe side, we're returning to Newark."

Okay, sounded all right to me.

At the airport on our approach, I could see the flashing lights of emergency vehicles lined up along the runway. Foam trucks were standing ready. It turned out one of the engines needed replacing. It had been more than just a minor problem.

Then there was a trip to Seattle when the turbulence was so great that the stewardesses had to remain strapped in their seats for most of the trip. Drinks and food could not be served. This experience brought back my fear of flying in full force.

While I was suffering, my wife, Carla, enjoyed the opportunity to sit back, relax and enjoy reading or just resting. She figured only one of us needed to worry. On long trips, she simply dozed off, while I had to keep awake to hold the plane in the air.

I learned that it is not uncommon for people who need a sense of control to fear flying. That I was not alone wasn't so obvious in those days. It turns out that fear of flying affects almost 20 percent of travelers. Telling us that driving a car is actually more dangerous does nothing to relieve our fear.

It turns out that an overactive imagination is a rather common commodity. Of course, knowing that the person sitting next to me was also near panic would have done nothing to calm me.

Now that I fly with impunity, there are many programs to help people overcome the fear of flying. They include virtual reality headsets that allow you to experience what you would see and hear on a flight, aiding in your desensitization while still on the ground.

For more information about overcoming a fear of flying, see www.anxieties.com and www.learn2.com.

Sailing on the Tall Ships

Not everyone is a candidate for the plush cruises on giant luxury liners. For those who think small and want the feel of rolling waves and salt spray in their faces, there are windjammer cruises. Windjammers are the tall sailing ships that take only a small number of passengers and "allow" them to help hoist the sails, coil the ropes and steer the ship.

Unlike passengers aboard giant luxury liners, windjammer guests don't dress for dinner, quickly get on a first-name basis with their shipmates, and never go to bed glutted from the midnight buffet.

Nineteen windjammers, four of them over 100 years old, sail out of Camden and Rockport, Maine. These are true sailing ships with old-fashioned amenities, taking from 6 to 40 passengers. Seventeen more modern windjammers carrying from 30 to 90 passengers sail out of Miami, Fla.

Years ago I sailed Penobscot Bay off the coast of Maine on the *Stephen Taber*, and later I did the Bahamas on a more modern sailboat. Checking the Internet, I find that little has changed except the prices.

Here are some excerpts from the log I kept while onboard the *Stephen Taber*, a 22-passenger 68-foot schooner built in 1871.

June 21: Well, anyway, here I am in a tight bunk aboard the *Stephen Taber* — and it's already an adventure. The people here in Maine call us "rusticators," people who come to rough it. My fellow passengers are a bit older and include some academic types. The captain, Ken Barnes, is an ex-professor of history who gave that life up to become a sailor. Full of stories, he makes a very entertaining host.

He has practically rebuilt the ship.... Used only for coastal sailing, it hauled coal and wood before becoming a passenger ship.

June 22: I note a fair amount of white wine and beer gets drunk aboard the ship. I have no need for a drink; the sea makes me feel slightly drunk anyway. The gentle rocking of the boat has a very sedative effect and almost puts me in a mild trance.

Oak water casks on board made from old Scotch whiskey barrels have charcoal inside to keep the water pure. With no extra water for washing, hands and faces are all we clean. If the weather is fair, we can wash our hair with seawater and lemon Joy. Weather is very windy and cool yet.

Away from the city lights, you can see the marvels of the sky in a way that you may have forgotten existed. The Milky Way is glorious.

June 23: A rainy day and then fog. We sat until 4 p.m. and then made a run for it and beat a storm out of port. I heard one captain chide another for not coming out of the port. The run we did make was very exciting, the winds being high and the waves very active. Everyone on board was delighted with the caper.

All of our cooking is done on an old wood stove by the captain's wife, Ellen. I baked this morning using her recipe for Newby bread — it uses a lot of molasses — the group really loved it, which is quite a compliment considering the really good food Ellen is serving. We had an excellent New England boiled dinner. Everyone is complaining about too much food but still take seconds and thirds. Becky was saying that next time; we'll all meet at the fat farm.

We get to hoist and lower sails, and I'm absorbing some seaman's lore, like learning port from starboard. Everyone laughs a lot, and you get the feeling these are people who are seasoned adventurers.

Despite the petite cabins, no water for washing, lemon Joy and salt water for hair, and no privacy, everyone is saying what great fun this is.

June 24: We have been racing with the Angilique, a 95-foot schooner — what a beautiful ship. The two schooners in full sail, side by side slipping through the water, give one a real thrill. Great breeze today and good sun, ideal for sailing. However, the temperature changes frequently, and it's off and on with the jackets and sweaters.

We're at McClathery Island and just finished our picnic on the beach—two lobsters per person, and I learned how to eat them with a rock as a breaker.

June 25: There was only a little breeze today. I was at the helm through some narrows and had to make a major change of direction, which gave me a chance to use the compass. The wheel has lots of play, so you really run it by big moves.

June 26: What little electricity we had gave out, so we flush the toilets by bringing up buckets of water from the sea. Everyone seems very helpful on that.

June 27: This group seems more closely knit than some others I've traveled with. We have a real rapport with each other, exchanging names and addresses and promising to send pictures.

Some of the women don't look forward to going back to work. Most of the group don't know how to explain what happened here. They feel they'll just have to say, "You had to have been there."

Of the 19 tall ships that make up the Maine Windjammer Association, the *Stephen Taber* is unique. It is the oldest documented sailing vessel in continuous service in the United States and is included on the National Historic Register. In Maine, prices range from $775 to $838 for a six-day cruise.

Prices in Miami are similar but there's a different flavor to the cruise: It's warmer, and you can spend time in the water snorkeling, on the beach shell hunting, or doing some serious diving.

Remember, these cruises are not for everyone. If you like your comforts and professional entertainment, stay with the big ship cruises.

But if you want to get close to the sea, and experience hoisting the sails and swabbing the deck, then you should consider cruising on a windjammer. It's as close as most of us can get to the olden days of seafaring.

Offbeat Travel

Elmer Fudd, Rhino Were Difficult but Memorable

On organized tours, I have found that most fellow travelers are pleasant, intelligent and congenial. After we have shared a major trip, it is not unusual for us to drop each other a letter or e-mail. Some travel companions, however, I would classify as difficult.

Often they are difficult because they cause the rest of us to be late or because their behavior distracts us from our purpose, whether it be sightseeing or listening to a presentation. It's as if they are functioning in a world somewhat separate from the rest of us.

Fortunately, in any group of 24 to 40 travelers there has never been in my experience more than two. I would like to share a couple of examples from my journal some years ago on a month-long Elderhostel trip in China.

One man became known as "One-Dollar Kelly," the Chinese term for, "You're late." It was never his fault, and the kidding by the others did nothing to change his behavior.

When we were ready to move, the group would shout, "Where's Kelly?" He had an Elmer Fudd face and an abstracted approach to life. It was difficult to tell what he was paying attention to because his questions to our tour guides came from somewhere in a space that the rest of us were not attuned to.

He was one of the people who was on half a trip, because he often wasn't paying attention except under some circumstances, such as when he had drunk sufficient beer.

At one of our stops at a Chinese Vocational School, where the students put on a performance for us, local beer was provided. Some of us didn't drink, and that left more for Kelly, who drank six cans. His eyes glowed as he focused on the performers - he smiled at each new act and found things to laugh about that the rest of us were missing.

Because we were given too many bottles of beer at most places, he was a good person to have at your table. You could get up without feeling guilty that all that good beer was going to waste.

As the alcohol content in his blood came down, his glow would diminish, and he could become easily angered. At one stop he had put his entrance ticket in his suitcase, which was locked in the storage compartment of the bus. When the agent needed the tickets, everyone else had theirs. The agent refused to get the bus driver to retrieve it. Comments from the other passengers upset Kelly, and he lashed out verbally.

He bragged about traveling light, having less baggage than the other passengers, but he kept misplacing the little he carried so he never had his passport, tickets or camera when they were needed.

"Talkative Charlie," a large, heavy-set man, was hard of hearing, a condition not unusual when you travel with a group of older people.

It was the way he dealt with it that made him difficult. When he was an artillery officer, he had found protective earplugs unmanly and something only a woman would use.

Charlie also believed that using a hearing aid indicated a weakness. As a result, he was also a man on half a trip since he didn't hear much of what was said.

He did a lot of talking, which kept him in control of the topics of conversation where he knew or could guess what was being said. At the first Chinese language session he kept the teacher talking about the price of gas 15 minutes into the session.

The group finally recognized what was happening and clapped him into silence. This did not stop him from interrupting speakers to raise questions about topics he already was familiar with and thus could be more comfortable.

He reminded me of a rhino - he doesn't see much but charges straight ahead - and is dangerous when challenged. He chewed out one of the other members of the group for some offense, completely disregarding the reactions of the audience.

Although annoying, these people, in retrospect, do add a bit of seasoning to the trip. On my last long tour there were no difficult people, so they aren't always an essential part of travel.

I Should Have Stayed Home

"One, two, three — lift!"

The canoe scraped ahead three feet, and I reset my feet, feeling for a secure position on the slimy rocks.

"One, two, three — shove!"

The aluminum bottom of the canoe scraped along another three feet. My brother, Lester, and I stopped and stared ahead at the next 30 feet of rock-infested stream, looking for the area with the highest water and lowest boulders.

"If we can move those two sticking up in the middle, we can make six feet on the next push," I said.

We positioned ourselves, fingers under the lip of the first slippery rock, and heaved. My 62-year-old, overweight brother grunted as it splashed back into place. We tried again. This time, the rock fell to the other side, clearing a little more space for our gear-laden canoe.

The James River of the Dakotas, the longest nonnavigable river in America, was fighting us. It had lured us miles into a deserted part of North Dakota, where we had not seen a farm or road in the last six hours. We had seen our last human three hours back, a fisherman stalking the great northern pike that frequent the wide, quiet spots.

It was those wide, quiet pools behind small dams that led us into our miserable situation.

The James twisted in a series of tight bends and rock-covered narrows that refused to let our boat pass without considerable exertion. Electric or barbed wire fences periodically spanned its width, keeping cattle on their respective farms. And there were many cattle, standing on the sidelines, staring at us with what must have been amusement. It's hard to tell with cows.

The sweat flowed off our faces. We developed a deep understanding of why we were carrying a gallon of water per day for each of us. The 95-degree sun beat down, uninterrupted by any sign of shade. The last tree we had seen was a lone cottonwood on the bank of the river several hours earlier. There was a stand of six more straight ahead.

We stopped there to rest, but the gaseous, rotting vegetation drove us back to the river. Choosing between nausea and sunstroke, we opted for sunstroke.

We felt exhausted and trapped.

"We can't go on like this," Les kept repeating. "I've had it."

Why, you ask, were two men in their 60s, one a Salvation Army major and the other a university psychology professor, engaged in this battle for survival? At that moment, I was asking myself the same question.

Frankly, it wasn't my idea. Lester had called me in January. He said he wanted to revisit the scene of our childhood.

"Let's start at the source of the James River in northern North Dakota and follow it to its entry into the Missouri at the South Dakota/Nebraska border," Les said.

The James River, or Jim, as we call it, runs 700 squiggly miles through the flat prairie. We had spent our childhood along its banks. Our house in Jamestown was only a few feet away from the river. The Jim provided us with boating and swimming in the summer and skating in the winter. Occasionally, it flooded us out, but that was a minor consideration, accepted as a hazard of living near the water.

Les often wondered about the river's source and what it was like farther up. As boys, we followed the banks north but never got beyond a day's walk. Now, 55 years later, he was saying, "Let's do it. We can take a couple of weeks and go from the beginning down to Yankton."

In March, he called and said, "Let's make it just a week. We maybe can't handle two."

In May, it was, "What do you think about four days?"

Between us, we did a great job of preparing the right materials. We had a good canoe with a small motor, tent, cooking equipment, food and the right amount of water. What we didn't do was our homework on the condition of the river. Nonnavigable meant no big boats, not canoes, right? After all, if there's water, a canoe can go there, right?

Where we entered the river, a farmer told us that the editor of the local newspaper had taken a canoe down it two weeks earlier. That sounded reassuring. What the farmer left unsaid was that the Jim had been at flood stage, six to eight feet higher than it was now.

During one period when we were actually moving through open water, Les said, "There's more water back here in the bottom of the boat than we're bringing in with our shoes."

"I don't really think so," I said. "It really pours off when we jump in. Bail it out; we'll be all right."

He bailed. Half an hour later, as we worked around some shallow, weed-filled water, he reported, "There's more water here, and we haven't done any jumping in and out of the river. It's coming in from some kind of break. The rocks must have done us in back there somewhere. I think we should get out of here. The first road or farmhouse we see, we'd better start looking for help."

We hit yet another dam. On the other side of this one, the river had disappeared. Only a series of potholes stretched in front of us. Our will to go on had vanished. We had a leaking canoe and no place to float it. At least our pride would be intact. It wasn't as if we would be quitting because we weren't macho enough.

After a sweat-drenched trek down a dusty road, we found Tor, a Norwegian farmer, who brought his truck through the fields to the top of the dam. Tor seemed envious of our willingness to take risks, to do something as crazy as we were doing. He suggested that the next day we start in Jamestown and work our way north. We agreed that after repairing our canoe, that's what we would do.

It was no improvement. For two days, we faced 100-degree temperatures, a fierce wind and torrential rains. We spent one night nearly sleepless in our tent as an electrical storm added to the mix. I just barely managed my panic when my brother said, "Those were awfully big limbs overhead," or "Did you notice that giant tree on the side of us? It looked rotten. If it came down on us, they might never find our bodies."

Exhausted and beaten, we worked our way back to Jamestown the next day. But as we parted at the end of our journey, Lester had a suggestion.

"I'll be taking my vacation the same time next year," he said. "We've got all the equipment now. Why don't we take off from Jamestown and head south? This time, let's make it a week!"

Offbeat Travel

Kentucky Cave Causes Claustrophobic High

LOUISVILLE, Ky. - Quite different from the comfortable trips Carla and I had taken previously to such caverns as Kentucky's Mammoth Cave and Branson's Marvel Cave, exploring the cave in Otter Creek Park near Louisville made us feel like real spelunkers.

As part of an Elderhostel hiking and nature program, the instructors had been telling us in the days before attempting the expedition about the difficulties and dangers involved.

These scare techniques turned out to be their way of cutting down on the number of us who sallied forth. If there had been more than 15 participants, it would have taken too long to push and drag the less athletic members of the group over the waterfalls and through the tight spots.

As instructed, we wore old clothes and beat-up shoes, looking much like a convention of street people. Inside the cave we immediately stepped into 55 degrees Fahrenheit water that came up over our ankles. It took about 10 minutes for our feet to become numb.

Soon we were wading in rapidly flowing water up to our knees. Because no light penetrates into these caverns, the darkness was total. The height of the ceiling changed constantly, so our hard hats were necessary for basic brain protection. We could anticipate a lower roof ahead of us by the clunk of the leaders' helmets.

Because only the most able of the group chose to come, the 3-foot waterfalls turned out to be no major problem, even for the group's oldest members. When we arrived at a keyhole, I at first mistakenly thought we were to crawl through the lower hole, which had water coursing through it. Our guides explained that much deeper into the cave, where we would not go, you would need to crawl though the water with just your nose out, but here we would just go through the slightly muddy, chest-high hole.

The entry to this keyhole was fairly large, but the exit hole into the next room was quite tight. We needed to get down on our chests and elbows to push ourselves out the other side.

Floyd, one of our more flexible members, was the first to enter the 10-foot-long cavity. Here is where my fear of tight places was worst. I felt I couldn't get a decent breath of air into my lungs as I pushed myself to the narrow exit.

Once we were on the other side of the keyhole, for some distance the walls were often close together. I found it a tight fit; I'm not sure how anyone wider than I am squeezed through.

Even deep in the cave, visitors had written on walls and ceilings with spray paint. Is this a need going back to our caveman ancestors or just a way to get a piece of immortality by leaving a record that we were there?

On our way out, we made better time. Either our skills of going through and over obstacles had improved, or our desire to get back into the light and out of the cold water was giving us additional strength and agility.

The entrance to the cave was covered with a locked screen, but I noticed that someone had pried the screen back from the wall to squeeze in. Our guide said that a young couple in shorts and with only one weak flashlight had gone in and were lost for three days. Luckily for them, they were found, only a bit worse for the cold and damp.

Evan, one of our guides, had been trained as a member of a cave-rescue team. He said they had practiced in this cave, and it had taken them 4½ hours to get their "injured" person out.

We all finally emerged, bedraggled but triumphant, and as bonded as if we had endured a more formal "outward bound" experience.

Offbeat Travel

FBI Study Opened Door to Look at Serial Killers

This column started out as a review of my sabbatical year in 1981-82, when I spent most of the year traveling to some unusual places. The story was progressing well until I came upon my notes about my experience with the FBI training program in Quantico, Va. This entertained me so much that I decided to do this column on that experience instead.

I had been researching sex offenders, which led to research on murderers. As a result, the police academy at the University of Missouri-Columbia hired me to run seminars on the psychology of sex offenders. They said they liked my work because I didn't sound like a professor. I suspect they meant I didn't use big words and sounded like I had really met the offenders I talked about.

In 1981, MU sponsored programs by FBI agents on sex offenders and murderers. The first was for the staff at University Hospital. The presenter was Robert Ressler from the behavioral science unit at Quantico.

His specialty was studying the men responsible for serial sex murders, such as "Son of Sam" David Berkowitz, Ted Bundy, Charles Manson, John Wayne Gacy and Richard Speck. He had interviewed them and was using the material to predict characteristics of murderers based on crime scene information.

The second program was at the police academy and presented by Roy Hazelwood, who detailed how to predict who had committed a rape or a murder. He was in charge of a service that allowed police departments to send the FBI a crime report. FBI personnel would predict age, family background and personal characteristics of a suspect, such as "lives alone within a mile of the crime." When in my talks with Hazelwood I indicated my research interest in this area, he invited me to visit Quantico and study with them.

Being essentially on leave for the year, I booked myself in with a friend in Washington, D.C., for a week to explore what was new since I had lived in the area. Then I went to Quantico for my week of training on how to profile murderers and rapists based on such things as the condition of the body, habits of the victim, crime scene pictures and the autopsy report.

Like fighter pilots and others I had worked with who are in risky occupations, the agents I met really enjoyed their jobs. It was like being around a bunch of 12-year-olds playing cops and robbers. No slight intended: My inner 12-year-old got a kick out of hanging out with them.

I found the academy to be like a small college; nine buildings were connected by glass hallways. The academy is 40 miles from Washington and seven miles from the nearest town. FBI trainees come in for an 11-week program. At that time there were 250 agents, 250 police officers and 250 students on campus. I received a student badge and free room and board.

As I met some of the women training to be agents, I felt it was the kind of job my second daughter would have enjoyed and done well. The pay struck me as very good. Beginning agents made what I did as a professor, and advanced agents made considerably more. Anyone teaching at the academy had to have five years of experience in the field.

I had individual instruction from the agents in the behavioral science units. This included an opportunity to practice by working on some current cases that police departments had asked for help to solve. It was a bit gory because they were rather free with the color photos and the police reports from the crime scene. I got a good idea of how the top men play Sherlock Holmes and how good they are at thinking like a criminal.

Ressler also let me see some of his filmed interviews with some well-known killers such as Bundy and Kemper. He also had some audiotapes recorded by the killers as they committed murders. This did give me some bad dreams.

I also met, but did not work with, John Douglas. In the movie "The Silence of the Lambs," the character Jack Crawford is based on him.

Although the subject matter was horrific, the experience was entertaining and educational. I went on to co-author a number of papers on sex offenders and murderers.

Years later, I had a week of training from FBI agents on how to handle a hostage situation, another difficult area of police work.

Wayne P. Anderson

Lumberjack Museum Lets Writer Step into Dad's Past

On a trip when I find a spot or a display that taps into some deeply personal aspect of my life, I always have an emotional reaction. I encountered one of those displays at the Depot, an unusual collection of several museums in downtown Duluth, Minn.

One small section of this large museum is the lumberjack museum. Here, examples of the tools and equipment of an earlier period are on display along with explanations for us amateurs as to how they were used.

Lending a special charm to the exhibit are the videotapes showing what things were like when the north woods were alive with the sound of saws and axes as the seemingly unending forest was turned into lumber for a growing America. Scattered among the tools are photos of dining rooms and work crews from that era.

The area has a special meaning for me, as my father and my mother's father worked as lumberjacks in the area. My maternal grandfather came with four brothers from Sweden in the 1880s and began his life in America sawing down trees in northern Minnesota before he homesteaded in South Dakota.

My father, as a young man in the early 1900s, had worked as a lumberjack in Minnesota before he took up farming in North Dakota. My father was in his late 40s when I was born, and one of the few pictures I have of him as a young man is a postcard of him in his lumberjack clothes. In the displays, I found myself looking closely at the pictures of work crews from the era, just in case.

Officially, the Depot is called the St. Louis County Heritage and Arts Center located in the Old Duluth Union Depot, built in 1892. Once a gateway for immigrants, the Depot is listed on the National Register of Historic Places.

The Depot's core and largest display area is the railroad museum containing old engines, cars and assorted railroad equipment from the 1800s and 1900s. The equipment is reconditioned and set up to be viewed so visitors can enter the cars and view the dining rooms, mailroom and engineers' cabin.

To add to the feel of that era, a street from turn-of-the-century Duluth is reconstructed along one side of the trains. The day I was there, Thomas the Tank Engine was running, so groups of children were running in and out of the engines and cars as they waited for the "all aboard" for Thomas.

In a side area of the Depot is a small but emotionally moving Vietnam veterans' museum. A film of veterans talking about their experiences in the war and what it was like to leave Vietnam and come home gives some insight into the effects of war on different people.

On two floors next to the trains is a children's museum with mostly scenes from children's stories. Children can dress in costumes of the period and have their pictures taken. An art gallery didn't warrant much of my attention, and the theater wing had no shows running on the day I was there.

The city of Duluth is picturesque. The streets are paved with brick in the downtown area but laid out so that they are smooth for driving. Above the major streets are walkways connecting downtown buildings, ensuring that no one has to go out during the cold and snow for which Minnesota is famous.

With its cobblestone streets, specialty shops, storefronts and related exhibits, the square around the Depot gives a historically accurate picture of 1910 Duluth. Your ancestors don't need to have ties to the area for you to enjoy it.

Wayne P. Anderson

Farm Creates Picture of Life during the Great Depression

Because I enjoy visiting historical villages, I'm pleased to see more are appearing around the country with appropriate memorabilia. Recently I saw a farm from a period I had not seen re-created before: Wellington Farm, USA, near Grayling, Mich., where it's always 1932.

The publicity folder says this is a "60 acre open-air interpretive museum designed to provide an educational opportunity for visitors to experience life as it was in rural mid-America during the Great Depression." As I was born on a farm just as the Depression hit and had done farm work as a kid, I quickly dropped back into a time of my own life.

Because I arrived early on a rainy day and was the only visitor, I had a personal guide to lead me around the farm. The young lady had been trained by the owner and was very knowledgeable about the equipment and farming procedures of that time. She introduced me to a number of things I hadn't known about, such as how to make a broom and how to run a family still to make alcohol.

The farmstead kitchen brought back memories of my mother and my early life — the old kerosene stove and lamp, the heavy irons like the ones she heated on the stove to use to iron clothes, the churn like the one I used to make butter. Other items were ones we didn't have, such as the ice box (we put perishables in a pail on a rope down the well) and the electric washing machine (ours was powered by my mother's arm).

The farm also has a blacksmith shop, a grist mill, a carpenter shop, sawmill and machine shed — a few more sheds than we had on any of the farms I knew as a child. The three thrashing machines were like the ones into which I pitched bundles of wheat, painful work that gave me the motivation to go to college. The steam engines that drove the mills and the carpentry tools were familiar to me.

The collection of animals was small: four goats, a ram, one cow and calf and a small horse. The goats brought back memories of the one that would chase my younger brother around the yard. What were unknown to me in the '30s were the three llamas, three emu and two peacocks. I'm not sure what they were meant to show, but they had never been on any farms I knew about. My guide knew the personality of each of the animals, including the chickens and two roosters that had to be locked in a cage because they insisted on pecking the visitors.

On weekends, re-enactors work the blacksmith shop, the grist mill and the lumber mill with other re-enactors in period dress available to discuss the '30s. The farm also puts on barn dances, tractor pulls and other program during the summer. The visitors' center was stocked with Amish farm-baked pies, jams and jellies and handmade toys.

I enjoy the opportunity to drop back into time and to touch those objects that meant so much to people in the past. For the modern generation of visitors, I believe this experience is much better than books for letting them know what another time and place was like.

Section 6

Exploring the Foreign Scene

On a Subject of Modest Importance

When traveling in Europe, after learning "hello," "thank you" and "please," the first phrase I memorize in a foreign language is the one for "Where is the toilet?"

Not the polite American "Where is the bathroom?" or "Where is the restroom?" Asking for either of those is likely to get you a dumb look or a "We don't have one here."

Instead, some form of the word toilet is common. It may be written "toilette," "tualeta," "toiletten," or something similar. You occasionally may see the word "kloset" or a sign with a large WC (water closet) on it.

Once you find the WC, there is frequently the amusing process of figuring out how to make it flush.

My family lived in Europe for several years, and my four daughters were enthralled with the mechanics of making toilets flush. Not only did those mechanics differ in different countries, even the toilets within a single city might have different flushing methods. By the time we moved to an apartment in Holland, we considered ourselves quite wise in the ways of toilet flushing.

Shortly after our arrival at the apartment, Carla called me to the bathroom.

"How do you flush this thing?" she asked.

Because the tank was high on the wall, the usual methods were out of consideration. There was no lever in front of the tank, no recessed button on the side, no knob on top. We examined the floor carefully for a foot pedal. None there. A pull chain, which is frequent in England, seemed the next-logical choice, but it didn't exist, either.

After considering all the possibilities that we knew of, Carla sat on the edge of the bathtub and I stood by the pipe leading down from the tank, trying to see what we were missing. I reached out to rest my hand on the pipe, felt it give and heard the rush of flushing water. Turned out you flushed toilets in some places by pulling down on the tank pipe.

Besides the challenge of flushing, there is the companion challenge of toilet paper. I recommend that you carry your own. You will frequently find that it doesn't exist. If it does, it may be like wax paper, sandpaper or newspaper. In some cases, it really is newspaper squares.

As one of my daughters said with a sigh, "I know we're in a foreign country. The money falls apart in our hands, and we can't tear the toilet paper."

In Greece or Turkey, you may find the plumbing cannot handle flushed toilet paper, so look for a special waste container. By the way, I found the same problem in Mexico and Ecuador.

To use a public restroom, when you can find one, usually costs the equivalent of 25 cents, so be sure to keep some local coins available. Once, in Portugal, Carla, with two little girls in tow, found herself in need of such a facility. But she didn't have any local coins. The determined attendant followed her quite a distance to my location so Carla could pay her.

I was disconcerted to find that, in many places in Germany and France, the female attendants in the men's rooms go about their cleaning while you are doing your business. Locals appear used to this lack of privacy. We Americans are a bit put off by it.

In some places, be prepared to walk into a squat toilet. You'll find two footprints and a hole in the floor. Squat toilets can take a bit of getting used to, and my daughters never did. They are routine in most Middle Eastern countries and are still used in parts of Europe.

My visits to Western Europe have been very short in recent years. I have been spending most of my time in Eastern Europe. So although I have yet to see one, I understand that automatic street toilets are the newest addition to the toiletry of Western Europe.

To use one, you put money in a coin slot and step into a freshly disinfected space that includes a wet toilet seat. You get 15 minutes to do your business, at which point the door automatically opens.

Never sneak into an automatic toilet while someone else is leaving. If you haven't paid, the toilet bowl will disappear into the wall, and you will be sprayed with disinfectant.

Toilets are a part of the travel adventure that is seldom mentioned, yet everyone needs them. So treat them as another chance to learn about foreign customs.

Wayne P. Anderson

Trips to the Twilight Zone

Every so often, I find myself in the Twilight Zone, where logic is suspended and I exist in a different reality.

No, it isn't drugs, but a combination of factors. Usually I'm tired, it's late and the setting is unusual. One such step out of reality occurred in a village in Spain on Good Friday many years ago.

We were living in Madrid and had a long weekend off in which to visit Seville for Holy Week. Our oldest daughter, 16, was left in charge of her three sisters in our sixth-floor apartment off Generalissimo Avenue.

In our naiveté, we didn't know just how crowded Seville becomes during Holy Week. When we arrived, the streets were jammed with floats carried by members of church brotherhoods, followed by a mass of spectators, winding their way through the streets in slow procession from their own churches to the cathedral in the center of the city.

There are 57 of these brotherhoods, each with its own life-sized, lifelike figures of Jesus and Mary carried on large floats. Many of the images were done by master craftsmen centuries ago, and much effort is put into dressing Mary in the most decorative robes.

The processions were continuous during the week. No sooner had one church done its part than another would take over. Penitents with pointed hoods to mask their identities marched behind the floats carrying crosses, and some flagellated themselves with whips.

All in all, it was one of the most impressive scenes we have witnessed. When we finally went to find a room for the night, no lodging was available. After dinner we decided to find a space in a park and sleep in our car. It was a restless night.

The next day, Good Friday, things were building to a crescendo, but we were exhausted. Early in the evening we decided to drive to a village in the vicinity that had a *parador* where we could stay the night.

Such was not to be: That, too, was fully booked. The clerk told us that they were to have their parade, and that it was a re-enactment of the Stations of the Cross. If we hurried to the town center, we would be just in time.

We parked outside the center and walked the narrow stone-paved streets to where we heard the action. Throngs of people were standing along the stone walls of the dimly lit streets.

It was then I was thrown into the Twilight Zone.

Tough Roman legionnaires appeared in their full battle garb, carrying torches. The metal on their uniforms clanked against their swords, and the reflections of their torches gleamed off the highly polished brass.

One soldier abruptly pushed me back against the wall. It was at that point that I felt myself falling back into time. I was suddenly in Jerusalem in the year 32 A.D. in a mob waiting for the man who claimed to be the Messiah to appear.

Then Christ materialized out of the gloom, the heavy cross on his shoulder. He was struggling to maintain his balance under its weight. His face was bloodied, and a trickle of fresh blood came down from the crown of thorns on his head. It was only after he had passed that I found I had been holding my breath.

I choked back tears. Further on, a woman came out of the crowd and wiped his face with a large scarf.

Those are the sharp memories. The rest of the experience has become a haze. I know we worked our way back to the car and then drove back to Madrid.

It was only later that I finally walked the Stations of the Cross in Jerusalem. Although it was interesting and I learned more detail about what I had witnessed in Spain, I did not experience the same sense of having been there.

Driving in Europe

In the past few years, my over-the-road travel in Europe has usually been with someone else doing the driving. When I have traveled in some underdeveloped countries, a hired driver was used. When Carla and I lived in Europe, however, we had our own car and got quite proficient at getting around on those roads. On trips my wife and I have taken since living there, we usually rented a car.

I was thinking about some of the problems of driving in foreign countries last month (1999) as with some anxiety I watched the driver hurl down a Croatian autobaum at 160 kilometers (96 mile) an hour. The real anxiety, however, came when we reached the two lane roads of Bosnia and I got to see what a high powered car can do in passing slower moving vehicles in oncoming traffic leaving only inches to spare between fenders.

I decided that there are times when it is very convenient and less anxiety provoking when traveling in Europe to do your own driving. Cars are easy to rent, and the rates are cheaper if you make arrangements before you leave the States. Some preparation is necessary to have a good experience.

Eight Considerations

1. Before you leave on your trip, I would advise you to have several things with you: full coverage collision and liability insurance and an international driving permit (I.D.P.) along with your U.S. driver's license. The I.D.P. is translated into nine languages and is easy for the foreign authorities to understand. Our drivers' licenses have information which are a mystery to foreign authorities since they indicate dates and measurements differently.

2. Check the rental car when you pick it up to be sure it has the required emergency gear consisting of a warning triangle and a first aid kit. Some countries also require a fire extinguisher. During winter driving you may need to have snow chains in your trunk. During a winter storm, when I was traveling from Italy to

Germany, I was stopped at the Swiss border and checked for the presence of chains.

3. Road signs are nonverbal and universal in Europe. Although many are self-explanatory, you should get a booklet and study it for any that may not be clear to you. You are expected to know and attend to the signs.

4. The first time I was stopped for speeding on the outskirts of a village, I was surprised to learn that you pay small fines on the spot to the arresting officer. Since you can't pay with credit card, check or American dollars, I recommend that you carry sufficient cash in the countries' currency. In the Balkans, by the way, the Deutsche mark is accepted almost everywhere, and in the European Union the euro is good. Speed limits are strictly enforced; and although the local people may violate them, keep in mind that you don't know where the hidden automatic devices are installed to monitor traffic.

5. In Germany, especially, you are expected to know the rules, and other drivers assume you know who has the right of way. Accidents are caused if you hesitate and/or get confused.

6. More so than in the states, never leave valuables in your car. Theft is more frequent in many parts of Europe than it is here. You are likely to find that valuables left in your car are not covered by your theft insurance. Most Europeans even lock their cars when they go into the station to pay for their gas.

7. Laws against drinking and driving are strictly enforced. You will notice that most Europeans do their drinking in pubs and cafés within walking distance of their homes. Legal alcohol blood level in some countries is a mere .05.

8. Unless there has been a recent war as in Kosovo and Bosnia, you will find the roads in much better condition than our own Interstate 70. They are kept very smooth and well cared for.

So why should you bother with your own car? There are many places in Europe that I would not have seen if I hadn't had my own car and the access it gave me to out of the way places. With a car you broaden the range of things you can see and open doors to adventure that a standard tour or use of the train cannot provide.

Bribery Part of the Paycheck in Corrupt Countries

When I was in Ecuador before a trip to Galapagos Islands, one of our guides in Quayaquil claimed with some pride that Ecuador was the most corrupt country in the world. What a strange thing to take pride in, I thought. But then it seemed to me that I had heard the same claim when I was in Moscow and in Pakistan. Who is right? And what difference does it make for the traveler?

Actually, Ecuador doesn't make the International Trade Association's list of top-10 corrupt governments, but its neighbors Columbia and Venezuela do. Nigeria heads the list as number one with Russia and Pakistan as four and five. Our neighbor Mexico makes the list as number six.

The widespread nature of corruption in these countries means more than just dishonest politicians at the upper levels placing relatives into positions of power. More important to the traveler it also means that bribery becomes an expected way of life for many governmental officials including those who are supposed to support the laws.

In a situation where the upper levels are corrupt, it becomes acceptable for everyone on down the line to also engage in dishonest acts. Under those circumstances, becoming a police officer or a customs or immigration official also becomes the pathway to an assured income.

The lower level government employees seldom get a living wage. They are expected to use the power of their position to raise the extra money they need to make ends meet. Where this is most likely to impact the traveler is driving, travel papers such as passports and visas and any goods that they are bringing into or taking out of a country.

Since most of us don't drive in third world countries, it's our drivers who get stopped. If the government check didn't come through for the local law enforcement, it will happen sooner rather than later. The laws are such that, if a person is arrested or given a summons even if you can beat the charge, it will take you so much time and energy that you search for a way out. The officer offers the out for a small fee, depending on how well heeled you look.

My impression in Russia and Pakistan was that bribes for driving offenses are rather straightforward and uncomplicated. There is no build up of the mark as there is likely to be in the case of passport or visa irregularities. Even if you have a valid visa, there are extra rules in terms of reporting your presence that you must follow. If in any way a rule is broken, you may be subject to a fine and in some cases imprisonment. This kind of threat provides a marvelous setup for some official to collect a bribe by helping you walk through the bureaucratic minefield.

Several years ago, a group I was with in Moscow ran into a problem with our visas, and as far as we could see, the officials kept changing the rules. It was taking considerable time for us trying to retrieve the passports. As the day for us to leave approached, the bureaucrat finally suggested that for a small extra fee he could expedite the solution in time for us to make our plane connections. The fee was small per passport, and I would have been willing to pay it the first day to avoid the hassle. Evidently, that wouldn't have built the stage for the final offer of help at which time the thankful pigeon shells out the appropriate fee.

Hey, it's a way of life. One that will continue as long as there is corruption at the highest levels and underpaid workers who are expected to take care of themselves with an outstretched palm.

How to Prevent and Survive Culture Shock Abroad

I'll never forget my worst experience with culture shock, had during a 5,000-mile journey throughout India.

I had lived in five European countries prior to this shocking experience. Our residences had been mostly in small towns, and we had adjusted well. Oh sure, when I lived in Germany I bellyached about their compulsiveness and their disdain of foreigners, but I enjoyed the year there. That successful experience, however, inflated my idea of just how much cultural change I could handle.

India taught me a lesson.

Travel ads I had seen promoting India were interesting, so it seemed like the next step for me on my quest to see the world. I signed on for a six-week tour at the most basic level: riding and sleeping on trains. I figured this would let me see the country without the barriers of fancy hotels and restaurants.

What a mistake.

The beggars, the poverty, the open sewers, the general filth, and different philosophy of life overwhelmed me almost instantly. The stress I experienced was compounded by a significant loss of weight (25 pounds) due to chronic stomach problems brought on by "Delhi Belly."

The effects of the culture shock I experienced continued long after I returned to the U.S. I found myself depressed and frequently on the verge of tears as I relived what I had seen. I was angry with people around me for being preoccupied with insignificant problems in the face of the bigger picture: overpopulation, food shortages, disease and early death experienced elsewhere in the world. In all of this I had a sense of powerlessness. I felt I could do nothing to change the world for the better. Even today, when I describe India to friends, I find myself choking up.

On the other hand, when I lived in Mexico for three months I didn't feel any culture shock. In part, this was because I was living with a doctor and his family. Although they only spoke Spanish, their lifestyle was not markedly different from what I was accustomed to.

Although culture shock is not entirely preventable, there are some things you can do:

- How close you get to the real culture makes a big difference. If you haven't traveled widely, start with organized tours of less than three weeks. The tour guides protect you, and more often than not, you will be staying in Americanized hotels and eating carefully prepared food.
- Have realistic expectations. Read up on the area and know what to expect. A prepared mind is good protection.
- Keep your sense of humor. I like traveling with British tour groups. They carry an air of superiority, and rather than get annoyed or weep they crack jokes about what is happening.
- Keep your sense of curiosity and wonder active. There are many new things to learn; be open to them.
- Recognize ahead of time that you will goof up. You will make mistakes. So many of us who travel have been successful in our home environments and fallen out of practice in how to fail or to do dumb things gracefully. Treat your mistakes as another learning experience, and don't be overly critical of yourself.
- Become aware of your limits. Traveling in Europe is not likely to stress most of us. On the other hand, traveling in a third world country, even for a short period of time, can deeply affect many people.

Meat, by Any Name, Makes his Meal

Recent television shows have scenes of people eating strange foods, sometimes in the wild for survival and sometimes on reality shows. I believe that is often done just to gross us all out.

Seeing what some people eat - grubs, worms, snakes, grasshoppers - reminds me that while hunting for food has not been a part of my family's lifestyle for many years, the culinary adventures on television bring back memories of animals I have eaten growing up and on some of my travels.

When I was a child in North Dakota during the Depression, my dad raised a variety of animals that could be eaten either by the family or sold. In 1934 we had lost the farm but rented a place on the outskirts of Jamestown, N.D., where my father truck-farmed to supply produce and meat for us and the local stores.

Around the barn, he raised rabbits, doves, chickens, guinea hens, geese, an occasional turkey and a goat. I don't remember ever eating the goat. The horses and the cow were working members of the family and not for eating.

When I was 8 or 9, my mother would say, "Wayne, will you get me a chicken for supper." I would chase one down, behead it and bring it to where she had the boiling water ready for plucking off the feathers and a sharp knife to do the rest of the preparation. That certainly introduced me to the hands-on nature of getting meat ready for the table, as did hog-killing time on my Uncle AG's farm.

During hunting season my older brother by 20 years would bring home duck, goose, pheasant and quail. A 12-gauge shotgun, a .22-caliber rifle and a .30-caliber rifle stood in the corner of most of my relatives' homes. I don't believe we had ever heard of people who were vegetarians.

When Cousin Johnny would come over from Montana, he sometimes brought different meats. I remember bear and antelope and some game that tasted like I was eating pine needles. Our local farming relatives would occasionally bring pork or beef, and I remember with what pleasure my dad would welcome mutton.

Although we didn't fish in the James River for anything but bullheads, during the winter my dad would buy a big box of frozen fish, and lacking an inside deep freeze, he would put it in a snow bank in back of the house. We would chop out what we needed for each meal.

In college, one of my professors regularly served horse meat because it was cheaper than beef, and college professor salaries were low. He didn't tell me it was horse until after I had eaten it.

Despite my variegated background, international travel sometimes introduced me to food that grossed me out. I remember ordering pheasant in England that had been hung in the cooler for 20 days that was supposed to be a special treat on New Year's Day. It tasted rotten to me. In Bosnia I was turned off at a special dinner given by the president of the University of Tuzla that included such delicacies as brain and kidneys.

Carla and I first ate squid and octopus when we were living in Spain. They were standard fares as tapas. The octopus was more like rubber bands in its taste and consistency.

In Africa, we ate zebra, ostrich and impala served using swords as skewers. I disliked the taste of ostrich, the zebra was tough but OK and the impala was very much like good beef. Some tourists were also fed elephant, eland and Cape buffalo.

In Australia, besides much beef and mutton, at various times we were served camel, kangaroo, emu and crocodile. Camel and kangaroo were a bit like beef, but I made no record of what crocodile and emu tasted like - probably chicken.

Carla and I have really cut back on meat as we have grown older, wanting smaller portions but also having some concern about how animals are treated. Despite this, my limits are seldom tested but could be - especially with what I hear about cats and snakes being served in some parts of China. Lewis and Clark's team, when they were on the West Coast for the winter, preferred dog to salmon. I would have to draw the line at dog.

Section 7

Experiencing the Mysterious and Unexplainable

Offbeat Travel

New Orleans: Its Unique Dark Side

New Orleans is unlike other U.S. cities. Part of the difference is a strong European influence from the Spanish and French who controlled its early history. Partly it's the scars left on the city from the tribulations it has had with weather, disease and war. The Big Easy, as locals call it, is a good city for conventions, classy vacations and gambling, and it's a stepping-off place for cruises and flights to South America.

But there is another side to the town that I find more interesting.

Although I have been there almost a dozen times, I have little memory of the newer parts of town. It's the French Quarter, the old plantations and the cemeteries I remember. More than in any other U.S. city, the locals are into walking tours, and these excursions are unlike those you find in other cities. Here you will find more registered ghosts than in any other city. New Orleans claims among its residents practitioners of voodoo, both dead and alive. Even before the imagination of Anne Rice produced novels about vampires, the city had more than its share of people who believed in them.

If you go, be careful — the living are more dangerous than the dead, and the crime rate is high. If you don't want to be mugged, it is recommended that you see the most interesting places with a guide on an official tour. Reports indicate that tour leaders at some of the cemeteries might be armed. The tours take place in the middle of the day when the sun is high and thieves and robbers are less likely to be hiding among the deteriorating tombs.

The Cemetery

Of the 42 cemeteries in New Orleans, St. Louis No. 1 is the most frequently toured. It has been around since 1789. At first, locals buried their dead underground, but when floodwaters came, which was frequently, they often found their relatives' bodies floating down a stream. They tried different kinds of coffins but finally gave up and began burying their dead in tombs above the ground. The rows of tombs with crosses and statues on top give the cemetery the feel of a small town built for dolls. It does look like a "City of the Dead."

A cemetery tour is also a tour of the history of the city and its interesting and sometimes odd residents. New Orleans was and is a deadly city in a number of ways, and markings on the tombs indicate that many of the occupants died from plagues such as yellow fever. In the city's early years, up to 10 percent of those in town during the summer months could expect to die from one disease or another. The city also was in the path of hurricanes, floods and other natural disasters.

Because death was so widespread, special rules had to be made for the graveyards. After a year and a day, the family could push what remained of the previous occupant to the back of the cavity and put in a new body.

Marie Laveau's tomb in cemetery St. Louis No. 1

The most publicized tomb belongs to Marie Laveau, the so-called queen of voodoo. Voodoo is a religion brought in by slaves that combines African rituals calling on the powers of nature and the spirits of the dead with aspects of Christianity.

Voodoo is still practiced in parts of the South and in the Caribbean.

Laveau, who died in 1881, was said to have been psychic, and tales abound of her amazing powers. She is given credit for being a creative genius in the ways she changed voodoo into more than a superstition.

When she died, a daughter took her place, and many people continued to think that she was the original. This unnaturally long life added to the mystique surrounding Laveau. This includes the belief that she returns to life once each year.

Her tomb is a special place for visitors to the cemetery. You will find offerings at her tomb and see people going through rituals to obtain her assistance. They chalk three Xs on the tomb, spin around three times to the right and three times to the left, then lean their heads against a stone wall and make a wish.

Voodoo

I haven't visited it, but for more information on voodoo, the Voodoo Museum is at 724 Dumaine St. in the French Quarter. There are shops selling voodoo supplies where you can get the concoctions said to bring success in business, school or love. If you don't want to bother, you can buy prepared *gris-gris* bags that are said to improve your luck. Voodoo tours also are available.

The practice of voodoo must have appealed to slaves who were subject to total control from their masters: With their rituals, they could call on spirits to give them some control. If the master was cruel, the slaves could make an image of him and take out their aggressions on the doll, hoping he would suffer pains in the same places into which they placed their pins.

Ghosts

Because of the relative youth of the people killed violently, the streets of the French Quarter are said to be filled with more spirits of the dead than of the living.

Wayne P. Anderson

Ghostbusters, parapsychologists and those attracted to mystery come here to make contact with spooks who are caught in perpetual re-enactments of their last moments on earth. According to local theories, those killed violently enter a zone much like that in the movie "Groundhog Day" — constantly reliving the day of their death.

Probably the most famous haunted house on the ghost tour is the LaLaurie House on Royal Street. Madame LaLaurie built the house in 1832, and the ghosts are said to be mostly slaves she killed in her attic torture chamber. Occupants report apparitions such as a large black man in chains who confronts people on the stairs.

Screams seem to be all that remains of some who died there, and people walking by report hearing them.

Three companies offering ghost tours have Web sites at www.neworleansghosts.com/, www.hauntedhistorytours.com, and www.**hauntedamericatours**.com/. There are more, but this gives you some idea of the popularity of the topic.

Offbeat Travel

St. Augustine's Ghostly Excursion

ST. AUGUSTINE, Fla. - The 11-year-old girl stands at the gate to the entrance of the old city section of St. Augustine, waving at the cars driving by. It's two o'clock in the morning and when a concerned driver from out of town phones the police to report a child unattended on the street, he is informed there is no such child and that he has just seen one of the many ghosts of the city. Some say the young girl was assigned to welcome visitors to the city. Others say she was warning people away because of the yellow fever epidemic that killed her.

My wife Carla and I were on a ghost walk on a luxurious winter evening with our British guide, Karen, who was decked out in an 18th century costume. As we had walked St. George Street earlier in the day, we had seen the sales booth for a ghost walk led by the Lady in White and one by a deceased sheriff who could talk about ghosts from personal experience. The ad promised that if he didn't show, one of his deputies would take on the task. Also advertised were buggy ride and tram ride ghost tours. For those interested in seafaring ghosts, there was a nighttime sail aboard a 72-foot-long schooner.

We had decided to take the "Original Ghost Tours of St. Augustine" because the ad said it had been featured on the Discovery and Travel channels. That gave it extra credibility for us.

St. Augustine is the third-most ghost-infested city in the United States. Only Savannah, Ga., and New Orleans have more. Why so many? Our guide, Karen, felt it was because there had been so many violent deaths here as well as the deaths of young people from diseases like yellow fever.

Violence? An example was the death by beheading of 200 French soldiers by the Spanish army that captured them on an island across the bay from where we were standing. Shrimp boat crews coming into the bay in the evening report they see the heads glowing green in the water and disappearing as they get close to them.

Karen emphasized that the energy the dead leave behind them builds up in particular places. She took us to an outside wall of the Castillo de San Marcos where the firing squad executions had taken place. We could see the hundreds of musket ball holes in the wall, many too high to be aimed shots. She said that was because if the person to be executed was a friend, a soldier was allowed to shoot over his head so he didn't have his friend's death on his conscience.

The energy at the execution wall was mostly gathered in one corner, and this had been established, Karen said, by several university professors with special infrared gear and other sensitive equipment.

The spot in the Castillo de San Marcos where three ghost soldiers appear

It seems there are a number of ways ghosts show themselves. One way can be as energy that shows up on special equipment; another way can be as forms that a camera, but not the human eye, will pick up. For example, people who have their picture taken in the graveyard might find in the developed picture some stranger in an old-fashioned costume sitting next to them.

Other ghosts appear in solid form for seconds doing some repetitive task, often what they were doing just before they died unexpectedly. This includes the three soldiers on the parapet of the fort who were loading their cannon just before it exploded and killed them.

Some ghosts are able to generate enough energy that they can appear in solid form and converse. Two children in 19th century dress with rotten teeth meet tourists on St. George Street, have a brief conversation and then vanish before their eyes.

We stopped by several bed-and-breakfasts that allegedly had ghosts. Karen said that most of the more than 100 establishments in the city have at least one resident spook but that most ghosts were friendly. They would show themselves by a caress on your neck or pat on your back. Some were occasionally photographed by someone taking a picture of an upstairs window at night.

What did we see or experience? Not much.

We did see an eerie ghost-like face appear on one of the tombstones when Karen flashed her light on it, but that was the extent of what we saw.

Whatever your beliefs about ghosts, this is a worthwhile tour. You will learn some history, see the old town under conditions not possible during the day and have a fun experience.

The haunted graveyard in St. Augustine

Offbeat Travel

Savannah Ghosts

I was looking forward to taking tours of the ghosts of Savannah, Ga., because the city has a reputation for being the most spirit-ridden city in the United States. It was ranked in several sources as No. 1 over St. Augustine, Fla., and New Orleans, where I have also taken some very impressive ghost tours.

If nothing else, Savannah seems to be No. 1 in the number of ghost tours available. Every visitor center had copious brochures offering tours such as "America's Most Haunted City Tour," "Eye Witness Accounts Ghosts," "Hearse Ghost Ride," "Sixth Sense Ghost Tours," "Ghosts and Gravestones" and "Savannah Haunted History Tour."

Carla and I opted for a walking history tour and learned much about the remarkable history of the city and got reports on the many sightings of faces in windows of empty rooms, thrown objects and colored orbs. Our young female guide had hoped our cameras would record some of the orbs since they indicated spiritual presence. The spirits weren't on call that night, even in one of the old moss-heavy oak trees in Wright Square where she said they almost always show themselves.

This square had one of the most frequently reported ghosts, especially by pregnant women and mothers. Alice Rey, an indentured servant, had drowned her abusive master in his bathtub. She asked for clemency based on being pregnant, but after giving birth to his baby she was hung here.

And although our guide told many interesting stories, something was missing. Was it her lack of costume? Her youth? Or was it in the stories themselves?

The next day we stopped at a visitors' center, of which there are many, and asked for suggestions. The guide said the best was the "Savannah Haunted Pub Crawl" that he had taken with visiting relatives and friends at least 100 times. He said to be sure to get the one starting at the Moon River Brewery. The strength of the tour, he said, was that it got visitors into the actual sites where the ghosts reside, thus increasing our chances of experiencing some of the paranormal phenomena.

The gallows in Wright Square

Wikimedia Commons

Our guide was dressed as a Civil War Confederate soldier, complete with sword and 1854 Colt revolver. We met in the second story of the brewery in rooms in very poor condition. They had been that way for years because when workmen would commence to make repairs and refurbish the area, strange things would happen — misplaced tools, workers feeling cold water down their backs with no water visible — and they would refuse to continue to work in the area.

I had wondered why Savannah had more reports of ghosts than the other two contenders for most ghost ridden, St. Augustine and New Orleans. After some thought I concluded the locals appear to be more sensitive to the presence of spirits than people elsewhere and show this by their refusal (inability?) to work in areas where spirits are present. I was also impressed with the consistency of what phenomena were reported, even by people who had not been forewarned about how this or that particular ghost showed itself. That is, the visitor could go into an area knowing nothing about the local spirits and report a similar experience to others.

Offbeat Travel

The guide, who had lived his 34 years in Savannah and had been leading groups as a sideline for eight years, had not only talked to people who had experienced paranormal phenomena in these settings; he had experienced some of them himself. We went to five more bars, our leader taking at least one drink at each. This might have helped him to tune into paranormal phenomena.

An Irish bar where the interior had been the set for the movie "Bloom" when it was filmed in Ireland was on the tour. The bar's owner had bought the set and moved it to Savannah. Its ghost was one who opened doors and walked up and down stairs to the basement. Evidently many of the bartenders had experienced this one. Because of the ghost or ghosts, the basement was left unfinished because workmen refused to work there also.

The next morning as I was waking up, it occurred to me why I was finding the tours unsatisfactory. The tours I had taken in other places such as St. Augustine and New Orleans had spoiled me. The guides not only had told me what the phenomena were — the noises, the taps on the shoulders, the physical appearances — they had emphasized who the ghosts were. They went into detail about the conditions under which the ghosts had died and gave explanations as to why they refused to recognize they were dead or why they kept repeating certain acts, such as the little girl in St. Augustine who stands on the corner at night directing tourists to keep away from the area because of the rampant disease in the area that had killed her.

The tour guides we had in Savannah were not as free with stories if they have not been authenticated. They emphasized firsthand stories often reported to them by the person who experienced the thrown object or felt the cold water running down his back. I prefer the stories with more detail about the real people behind the ghosts.

Savannah continues to be a favorite place for ghost hunters who authenticate the various phenomena, and the guides take pride in reporting the facts. The bookstores also carry the largest number of books about the ghosts of the city than any of the other cities I have visited.

I had wanted to take one more tour to see whether it would finally meet my expectations, but Carla, who has less enthusiasm for ghost tours than I do, said two were all she could stand and she preferred we explore other options with our remaining time.

Savannah's Wright Square

Tower of London Ghosts

Because I toured the Tower of London during daylight hours the ghost tour lacked the atmosphere of the other London ghost tours that take place during the night. Still the Tower of London is an exciting place to visit if you want to experience the most haunted place in Britain: one that is loaded with famous names. It seems that people who got in the way of what the king wanted often ended up as ghosts.

The Tower has been around for 900 years and when you visit it you get a fascinating but dark side to English history. The Tower had a prison for the famous and was the site of beheadings, murders, torture and hangings.

Tower of London on a busy day

Our guide paid a lot of attention to the ghost of Queen Anne Boleyn who was accused of infidelity by Henry VIII when he learned that she had just had a stillborn boy. He wanted a wife who could have live boy babies, and since divorce was out of the question she was beheaded. At the chopping block you are told about how her headless body is seen moving through the chapel to her grave under the altar.

During the tour I got the feeling that being queen at times could be a dangerous job. Catherine Howard's ghost has been seen screaming for help in front of the room where she was kept before her execution. The headless body of Queen Anne is seen walking the corridors of the Tower. I wasn't sure how the viewers knew which queen was which since several of the ghosts were headless.

Chopping block at the Tower of London

Several of the stories are particularly gruesome. King Henry VIII had the 70-year-old Countess of Salisbury, the last of the Plantagenets, sent to the chopping block. She refused to put her head on the block and ran away with the executioner hacking at her with his axe. The report is that her ghost reenacts her death with the shadow of the falling axe being part of the gory ghostly scene. Lady Jane Grey, who was only 17 when she was beheaded, has been seen on the battlements on the anniversary of her death.

On another tour of the Tower I visited the rooms of Sir Walter Raleigh, who was imprisoned in the Bloody Tower. Famous for explorations of the new world he got along well with Elizabeth I, but fell out of favor with her successor, James the First. He was imprisoned for some years, but eventually the King decided to execute him. Raleigh's last words on going to the chopping block are famous, "This is a sharp Medicine, but it is a Physician for all diseases and miseries." The reports are that his ghost looks like his portrait that still hangs in the Bloody Tower.

Also residents of the Bloody Tower are the ghosts of 12-year-old King Edward V and his 9-year-old brother, the Duke of York. They are seen wearing the white gowns that they were probably killed in. One other ghost that demands to be recognized is Sir Thomas A. Becket, who defied Henry II whose knights killed him at Canterbury Cathedral. I am not quite sure how he ended up being a ghost at the Tower. He by the way was the first ghost seen there.

Other ghosts also haunt the Tower, including some animals from the zoo that once existed there. I find the stories of the people who have seen the ghosts interesting, for example, the guard who saw a ghost so real he charged it with his fixed bayonet and went right through it falling and striking himself unconscious. The Salt Tower, a very old section of the complex, is so haunted that we were told the Yeoman Warders will not go into the area at night.

There is so much to see at the Tower and it is so loaded with history that it worth the visitor's time to take more than one kind of tour. I've taken at least four maybe five tours of the tower learning something different each time.

Wayne P. Anderson

The Tower of London

London Ghosts

You don't need to believe in ghosts or the paranormal to get cold chills down your spine and find the hair on your arms rising when you take a ghost tour. The ambiance is usually enough to convince even the most doubtful that they are in the presence of unexplained mystery.

I have lived in London, where there are more than a dozen ghost tours, which I suspect is more than any other city. The walking tours I have taken took place at night, with lighting provided by a lantern that cast long, creepy shadows and left the corners dark. The groups were usually led down dark old streets surrounded by buildings from the 18th century.

Typically, our guides were dressed in costumes appropriately macabre. If the tour had been around for a while, the stories were well rehearsed, and I would find myself checking the people walking next to me to be sure they were real and not spirits making a temporary visit to their old haunts.

I found it amusing that in London these residual ghosts are often seen from their calves up because after they died the buildings were modified, and the ghosts are still walking on the floors they were familiar with in life. Some of these ghosts only show up on the anniversary of their death.

The British take pride in the number of ghosts they have; for example, the Tower of London has enough ghosts to have its own ghost tour. What's so neat about that one is how famous their ghosts are. Imagine in one place the headless ghost of Anne Boleyn, Thomas Becket, Lady Jane Grey, Sir Walter Raleigh, and the princes of the Tower: Edward V of England and Richard, Duke of York.

In keeping with the Brits fascination with horrible crimes there are "Classic Murders and Crimes" advertised as "welcome to the nightmare factory …to the dark side of the most civilized city on earth."

Wayne P. Anderson

The most frequently taken horror walk visits places where Jack the Ripper left his bodies and goes into detail about their condition. I took that walk years ago and found it a little over the top for my taste.

London probably has more ghosts than any other city. In fact we don't remember anyone in Madrid, Rome or Paris ever mentioning ghosts as a regular part of the tourist trade. When I was teaching for the U.S. Air Force in England in 1972-73, I was surprised that many of the American personnel living in four- and five- hundred-year-old houses on the economy seemed to have had experiences with ghosts since coming to Britain.

London turns this national resource into a major attraction with a different ghost walk every night of the week with titles like "Ghosts, Gaslight & Guinness" and "Apparitions, Alleyways & Ale." The implication of those titles is that it helps explore this realm of spirits if you have imbibed a pint or two of ale. My favorite is the Tuesday night "Ghosts of the Old City."

Our guide took us to old houses, churches and graveyards where the London ghosts tended to hang out. We started near St. Paul's Cathedral where we were told about the ghost that walked through the wall of the Cathedral. The point where the ghost disappeared was found to have a secret door.

Even St Paul's Cathedral has a resident ghost.

I learned a lot of London history during the walk about plagues, the Great Fire, the terrible punishments for crimes and where the famous hung out. One of the pubs we visited was a hangout for body snatchers who created their own corpses to sell to medical students who needed a cadaver to learn anatomy. Evidently digging up graves was too much work.

The atmosphere in the old alleyways and courtyards adds a special flavor to the tales the guides tell. With the shadows and narrow alleys you can feel the still active spirits just a little ways into places where you cannot see.

In daylight haunted places are quite benign.

Fort George
The Most Haunted Place in Canada's Most Haunted Town

The drum and fife corps at Fort George in Niagara-on-the-Lake in Canada puts on frequent demonstrations of orders conveyed to soldiers by drum and fife.

NIAGARA-ON-THE-LAKE, Canada - Seeing re-enactors dressed in costumes of a previous era and reinhabiting a historical site always allows me to happily drop back in time for a taste of life in an earlier period, if only for an afternoon.

At Fort George at the entrance to Niagara-on-the-Lake in Canada, Carla and I were greeted by a re-enactor dressed in a red wool coat and white pants on a warm July day. When we asked him how he stood the heat, he said that after 27 years, he found it comfortable and didn't understand why we risked skin cancer in T-shirts and shorts.

Fort George has been reconstructed to resemble its appearance at the beginning of the Revolutionary War, with upright logs for walls and great reliance on ditches for protection. The system didn't work well, and the fort was rather easily destroyed by the attacking American revolutionary forces.

We found the fort to be well staffed by costumed actors placed in each building to answer questions and relate the history of the area. We had noticed that all explanatory signs were in French and English. One of the costumed women informed us that speaking both languages is a requirement for being hired. Many of the attendants looked young, and I suspect they were mostly students employed for the summer.

Two demonstrations are given at regular times during the day, one by a drum and fife corps and one by a group of musketeers. The leader of the drum and fife corps said he had been with the fort for eight years, but the rest of the group looked to be in their teens and were mostly girls. Nevertheless, it was an excellent demonstration of the orders conveyed to the troops by drum and fife, and we heard some popular melodies of the day.

I had seen the musket demonstration a few years earlier, so we skipped that, but my memory is of the visiting boys being enthralled watching old flint muskets being loaded and fired. In the officers' kitchen an older lady and a mother and her 8- or 9-year-old daughter were demonstrating cooking on an open-hearth log fire.

The marked differences in treatment were great between enlisted men and the officers, who often came from rich families and bought their commissions. This was shown in punishment, housing and food. The guardhouse had small, dark cells; outside was the punishment triangle, to which the man to be punished was tied and whipped with the cat-o'-nine-tails. An officer's offense, which would lead to dismissal from the army, would be one for which an enlisted man could be executed.

Original equipment from the time is displayed throughout; the re-enactors are well-versed in knowledge about the artifacts.

The fort's arsenal

Not content with a daylight tour, Carla and I went back that evening for the Phantoms of Fort George Ghost Tour. At the beginning our guide noted that Niagara-on-the-Lake had more ghosts for its population than any other city in Canada. Most of the local ghosts seemed to hang out in taverns. Ghosts are not restricted to taverns and the fort; earlier we had taken a tour of the Shaw Theater in Niagara-on-the-Lake and our guide pointed to a light on the stage. "That's the ghost light," she said. "Most theaters keep one burning at night when the theater is empty. When you don't have one, strange things happen. It's as if a bad spirit comes to visit and breaks or messes everything up."

At Fort George thirty-five of us were led by a cloaked guide with only a candle in a glass box. When he led us into darkened buildings, this did lead to eerie sensations and an overreaction to strange sounds.

Our guide had us looking for a 7-year-old, barefoot, blond girl to join our group, ghost hands on our shoulders when we went through a 60-foot-long, pitch black tunnel, and a face in the window of block house No. 1 as we passed it. We were not disappointed when none of the apparitions appeared.

The strangest and most frequently reported ghost was one that arrived in a fancy mirror. On occasion, visitors looking through the window to the officers' quarters could see an upper-class woman in the mirror brushing her hair. The guide suspected the woman had died shortly after her arrival. More recently, the viewers who can see her report she is standing outside of the mirror rather than just being reflected in the mirror.

Even though none of us saw any spirits on this trip, I found the visit to their haunts exciting, and, given the storytelling power of our guide, I got my fair share of chills down my spine.

Chinese Rites Keep Evil Spirits in Check

The ceramic figure of the Chinese man with a wicked, satisfied smile on his face captivated me. He had his arm in a large jar and his head was turned toward me as if to say, "See, I knew I could do it." I was in a Friendship Shop in southern China, and although I don't usually buy much in the way of souvenirs on my trips, this 7-inch tall figure attracted me; it was if he was expressing a side of my personality.

The clerk informed me the ceramic was a ghost or evil spirit catcher. His story indicated that Chinese homes are always in danger of becoming infested with spirits who do mischief and cause unpleasant things to happen. Fortunately, talented people exist who can capture them, place them in a jar and remove them to a place where they will do no more damage.

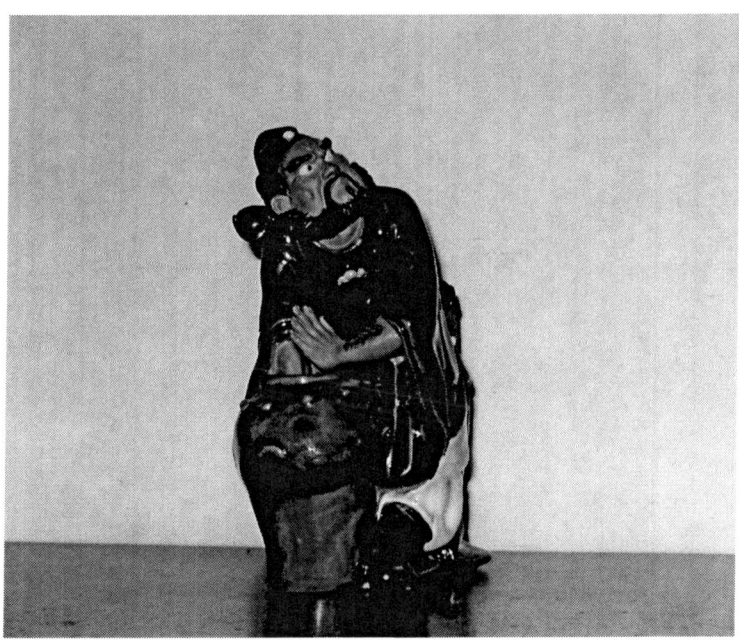

Chinese ghost catcher

That sounds a lot like our movies about Ghostbusters, but evil-spirit-catching was a going business in China a long time before Bill Murray was apprehending apparitions on the big screen.

After a bit of required dickering about the price, the ghost catcher was added to my collection of ceramic figures on a shelf at home that represent aspects of myself. He represents the therapist in me who helped clients deal with the psychological ghosts or evil spirits of their pasts.

Some years later, in 1993, my wife Carla and I were in a Beijing shop where a young man was carving fright masks in wood. The artist said these distorted faces were intended to be put on the outside door of a house to prevent evil spirits from entering. One mask now hangs on the wall of my office.

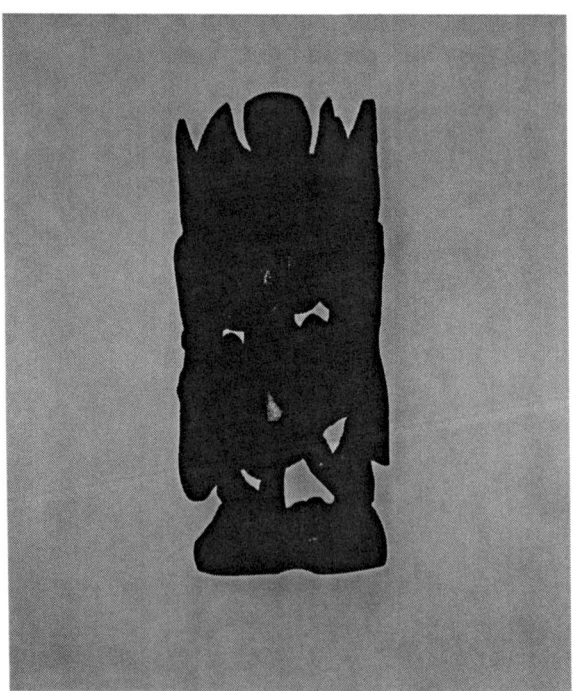

This mask placed on your outside door keeps evil spirits out.

As we toured places such as the Summer Palace, we were asked to watch our step to avoid stumbling on the threshold of the door. Evil spirits had a policy of only going in straight lines and would not be able to get over a raised threshold. It became clear to me that these were pretty limited evil spirits. They could be caught, were frightened by masks and couldn't get over a hump a 3-year-old could master.

The theory, as close as I could understand, was that when people die, the good part of their spirit goes to nirvana and what was evil in them gets left behind. Although this evil aspect of self has limitations, I kept hearing that care must be taken in dealing with these invisible but dangerous pests.

There are other methods to keep one safe from harm, including the following:

- Wear new clothes on New Year's Day so the evil spirits won't recognize you.
- Have a huge dragon parading in the streets to scare away the ghosts.
- At weddings use lots of firecrackers because evil spirits don't like loud noises.

So if you happen to have Chinese evil spirits acting up, you have a multitude of techniques to limit their powers to harm you.

Wayne P. Anderson

Ghosts of Williamsburg

When I took a ghost tour of old Williamsburg, Virginia, late last summer, the number of tourists was so large we were divided into two groups. Meticulously citing his sources, my group's guide was a professor, a good storyteller but one who was adamant that he didn't believe in ghosts. This was an interesting contrast from other ghost tour leaders I have encountered who have at least been open to the possibility of ghosts. The other group got a leader who frequently jumped at a participant with the equivalent of a "boo" causing all the members to scream.

My group had a pleasant nighttime visit to Williamsburg with more than half of our guide's stories being a straightforward history of the community without the supernatural element. We started at the College of William and Mary where we stood at the statue of Lord Botetourt in front of the two oldest buildings on campus, one being the oldest existing academic building in the US.

The latter building is no longer used as a residence because of the number of ghosts in it. One of them is a young Indian boy who lived in the building at a time when Williamsburg was trying to improve relations with the local tribe by taking their children in and training them to be white. The children had to wear woolen clothes, eat white man's food, and behave themselves. This boy would escape at night and run naked through Williamsburg. He died from some English disease, but his ghost continues to be seen running through the streets at night. In places that are built up, his body is said to be half buried in the ground as he runs since he doesn't recognize what has been done to the area since his death.

Of course the town looks different at night, but not ghostly. On the lawn in front of the Governor's Palace we were told of the nine-year-old who played with a friend there, committing much mischief. The boys died and continue to be seen at night jumping over the wall and playing with their hoops. More importantly the nine-year-old had been in the third grade and now third grade children at the school find papers rearranged or torn and other tricks done. Here they don't say the dog ate my homework; they say the ghost got into it.

Earlier in the day when I had visited the Peyton Randolph house, ghosts had not been mentioned. Our professor said the building is regarded by some people as the most haunted house in Williamsburg. One of the ghosts is a woman who seems distraught and appears in front of one of the beds. One woman who saw her was able to stay the night, but another couple ran out and never came back.

Some ghosts make their presence known through sounds or opening and closing doors. In one house the door would open and would not stay closed. After a skeleton was found in the attic and removed, the door stayed closed.

The house that has the most paranormal phenomena is the George Wythe House. Cold spots, lights, the sound of chains and an apparition or two. Ann Skipwith, a former resident who died in childbirth, is the ghost most frequently seen. She is dressed in an evening gown and when people approach her she vanishes.

George Washington used the Wythe House as headquarters before the Yorktown siege, and Thomas Jefferson and his family lived there at one time.

Our guide explained the use of oyster shells while we were standing on one of the walkways embedded with crushed oyster shells. The shells help prevent muddy walks and give a light covering that enables walkers to better see the path at night.

At the end of the tour I felt fortunate that I had been placed with the guide that suited best suited my interests, leaving me both informed and entertained.

The George Wythe House is probably the most haunted house in Williamsburg.

Missouri Boasts Scores of Scary Tales

In the early 2000s I become aware of the number of ghosts said to hang out in Missouri. Intellectually, I don't believe in ghosts, but when I am in a place and a guide is telling the story of how a ghost came to be there, cold shivers run down my back. I believe people see, hear and feel things for which I have no explanation.

Over the last ten years I've taken several tours with other writers looking at Missouri history in the western part of the state. My first awareness that ghost stories abound here came in St. Joseph. This faded beauty of a town must be a comfortable one for ghosts, given the number of them that are said to haunt the area.

A number of the old homes that have been restored as bed-and-breakfasts have their private spooks, only some of whom you will be told about. It depends on whether the owner sees it as an attraction. Even the Pony Express Museum has a young rider — who lost his life during the service's short existence — who comes around to haunt the old office.

Near St. Joe is the Jesse James family home. Although ghost hunters didn't find any evidence of spirit life, staff members at the museum say they have been present when doors slammed shut on their own and lights were seen moving around in the locked house. Others have felt a menacing presence so strong they refused to stay there alone. Occasionally the spirits of restless horses have been heard in the woods near the house.

Also connected with the James family is the old Jackson County jail, where Frank James was held after his arrest. The ghost doesn't appear in person, but some people hear his footsteps and feel his cold presence in one of the cells. The guides say visitors who don't know which cell contains the ghost can pick it out, guided by the threat that pervades the room.

Wayne P. Anderson

Haunted jail cell in Independence, Missouri

Excelsior Springs, outside of Kansas City, claims a number of sites with ghosts. I stayed at the Elms Resort and Spa and was taken on a tour by a staff member who claimed the resort had seven ghosts, but unfortunately she didn't know who any of them were.

That was a disappointment to me; if I had that many ghosts in my place of business, I would capitalize on it.

Later, while in the lap-pool area, she remembered one of the ghosts. It's a woman who walks around looking for her lost child. She bothers people who swim alone by pulling their hair and throwing things across the room.

At Wilson's Creek battlefield outside Springfield, we were told that people have seen ghosts of Confederate soldiers and heard strange noises — as if soldiers were walking and talking in the woods.

Jesse James home

In the stories I have heard, ghosts don't often show up in person; instead, they tend to make noises, form mists, turn on or create lights and produce cold spaces that fill people with dread. I imagine that when I encounter a ghost who looks real, who walks up, looks me in the eye and then vanishes, I would become a believer.

Local author Joan Gilbert has written a fascinating book, "Missouri Ghosts." She has some particularly good stories about ghosts in my home town of Columbia and surrounding towns.

I suspect that in certain sections of the state with a dense ghost population, ghost tours will become a tourist attraction. Until then, I'll just enjoy the cold shivers on those occasions when I have a guide who says, "We have our own ghost in the house. Let me tell you about her."

Wayne P. Anderson

The Elms in Excelsior Springs, outside of Kansas City, claims seven ghosts.

LaVergne, TN USA
09 February 2011
215885LV00003B/1/P